SYNARCHY

THE COMPLETE GUIDE TO THE ELITE GROUPS
THAT RULE THE WORLD IN THE 21ST CENTURY

RESEARCHED AND WRITTEN BY
AMY SAYS WTF

"If you are lucky and work hard, you will find some truth. If you are lucky and work really hard, you might find the WHOLE truth. If you are phenomenally lucky and really work your tail off, you might find the REAL truth. But no outsider, EVER, learns the **WHOLE REAL TRUTH**."

This book is dedicated to my sons, Jack and James

May you always be free...

INTRODUCTION

As far as I'm concerned, these demons should be executed for their crimes against humanity. What they did to the world in 2020 is so remarkably evil it is too hard to actually sit and think about it without wanting to go mad. The coronavirus psychological operation abrupted the lives of so many, killed so many and broke the spirit of so many. Businesses lost, lives lost, minds lost. These people, if you can even call them people, have been pulling the strings behind the scenes for centuries and the takeover of America started a long time ago.

In the 21st century our world needs prayer more than ever. We are in a war and it could go on for years but keep in mind the world works in cycles and after war there is always a golden age that follows. What we are up against is so powerful but, in my mind, good always wins. The most fantastic thing that happened in the year 2020 is that the veil of evil was lifted and so many people have woken up to the madness that was always lurking. Everything is in plain sight now and there is no denying it. From the symbolism to the predictive programming to the fake news it is so easy to see if you want to see it. Some people still aren't ready and that's okay. I believe individual awakening happens when you least expect it and in your own way.

Many souls were called upon to raise the vibration on earth and you may have been one of them. Since June of 2019 you may have experienced extreme toxic and negative situations which forced you to be more authentic. I personally feel like I experienced this in my own life this year. And I hear all the time that people have lost friends or family relationships have suffered due to their own convictions and beliefs. This is your authenticity coming out. This is your awakening.

It is important to understand that we are energy. We are vibration, we are pure spirit. And we have a soul which is our core intelligence. Our soul directs our thoughts, feelings, creativity and our divine will. Words and intentions whether conscious or not can directly or indirectly form our reality. The more aware you become of your energy and the power to create the more successful you can be. When you block yourself from this energy it can cause frustration or a victim mentality. You might be one to make excuses about everything. But the point is during this shift or awakening you can start to be more aware. Being aware is the first step. Breaking out of the matrix and seeing the world for what it really is.

I believe we are in a constant dance and rhythm with multidimensional cosmic energies and planetary movements. December 21st, 2020 was not only the winter solstice, but Jupiter and Saturn were the closest they have been in 400 years, appearing right next to each other known as the Great Conjunction. I have been studying Vedic/Esoteric and Tropical astrology for almost two years, so I have learned an immense amount of astrology and it is just fascinating.

> *"Millionaires don't use astrology, billionaires do." – J.P. Morgan*

Jupiter is a leader planet who is associated with health, wealth and having a good time while Saturn favors setting limits and responsibility. When they collaborate like this you can expect major power struggles over the best way to **RULE**. On a macro level it is likely to bring about a cultural movement where things change in a way that they cannot be reversed, whether we want it or not. Which really falls in line with the great reset narrative. And in my opinion, this power struggle is between the Black Nobility feudal system and America.

What makes this conjunction different is that it is in the sign of Aquarius which is the sign of social change and justice for all. We had a preview of Saturn in Aquarius back in May of 2019 with the murder of George Floyd and the emergence of Black Lives Matter. Interesting that we have entered into the Age of Aquarius. The great conjunction of Saturn and Jupiter is happening at zero degrees, which signifies a completely new beginning. Each sign in the zodiac has 30 degrees, so if it were at 25, we would be starting to see the end of an era. But with this conjunction being at zero, we are seeing something new emerge.

As the world has been challenged to wake up and grow with the internet and the sharing of ideas, I believed some of us reached the fourth dimension while others lagged behind. When you understand that the concept of time is just an illusion, you have reached 4D. There are people still in the time matrix that worry and hurry, in-regards to time. The 5D influence has been accelerating everyone's energy whether you know it or not. I do believe in synchronicity, signs, divine messages and non-physical communication. I have ESP and I learned to trust my intuition as a sixth sense. Everyone is capable of this!

What are the symptoms of ascension? People have reported experiencing headaches, dizziness, migraines, ringing in the ears, heart palpitations, blurry or sore eyes, anxiety, clumsiness, inability to sleep or waking up repeatedly between 2-4 AM, relationship strains, body heat, sore muscles, a strong desire to find purpose in your life, greater forgiveness and empathy, lethargy, change of diet, ending or shifting of friendships, increased telepathy, noticing triple digits on the clock for example seeing 333 or 444, gaining an interest in all things spiritual as in meditation or learning about esoteric knowledge, increased emotions or uncontrollable crying, feeling hugely inspired or creative, sinuses, back pain, shortness of breath, feeling that everything you've ever known is a lie, growing in your own personal power, and feelings of unexplained sober euphoria. Have you experienced any of this?

3D living is represented by fear, limitations, suffering, being locked in time and space and feeling as if you are working hard but getting nowhere. And 5D feels effortless experienced by forgiveness, unconditional love, being supported by energy, manifesting a positive reality for yourself and seeing your life's purpose start to unfold. Now whenever I would hear people talk about their life purpose I would scoff and roll my eyes because I was lost. But over the years and growing up I discovered strategies that got me on the path to where I am today. And some of them were by small acts of kindness to strangers, putting myself out there, having conversations with new people, and the most important was exploring my interests and running with them. I believe it is the 3D realm that keeps people obsessed with money and working around the clock and they don't have time to pursue their own hobbies or what makes them happy as an individual. It's time to break out of this 3D matrix.

It is so important to live your life with good intention, release toxicity, release bad relationships, and find ways to explore your own consciousness because for whatever reason, we were not taught how to do that, but I believe it is one of our missions on earth to rediscover. The elite groups of the world view us as rodents. We are not worthy of existing. They want to depopulate the planet and rid the planet of our existence. Sad but true. I believe we are at a turning point in humanity and it is up to us to be aware of these groups and realize that they don't have power over us. We have the power, and it starts with understanding who these groups are, not participating in their psychological operations and political theater and stop living in **FEAR**.

There are some alternative media outlets that want to blame everything on the "Jews" or "Zionism". They seem to repeat the same themes over and over again without taking into consideration that Disney, Murdoch and Hearst families are not Jewish, but they are some of the most powerful families in the world. There are plenty of Zionist criminals in the world, but they are not the only criminals and I would argue that the Zionists are not at the top of the pyramid. These Zionists work for the top. There was an article the other day claiming that Elon Musk was the "richest man on the planet" surpassing Jeff Bezos. It's headlines like this that make me scoff. Why don't you try the House of Saud, House of Braganza, House of Guelph or House of Habsburg? These are the power houses. These are the trillionaires.

In order to understand why every aspect of our lives have been infiltrated including our own government it is important to break down the most powerful groups in the world. This book attempts to unveil the truths of each group, think tanks and elite organizations so you can start to understand how they have been working together for centuries all the while fulfilling bible prophecy and what the new age will bring.

There are bloodlines that have claimed the right to rule since the beginning of time. These bloodlines have created think tanks and international organizations that are closed to society where they meet annually to regroup and plan their world agendas. This is no longer a conspiracy. These groups exist and have operated in plain sight since the 19th century while the rest of us work, raise families and struggle to get out of the financial debt slavery they have created for us. They are responsible for all of the psychological operations from 9/11 to social media addiction to coronavirus. Each one has been orchestrated to beat us down and strip away our God given freedoms. One by one this has been slow trickle of change, infiltrating and ruining our lives. It is possible to fight it. Turning off the news, not engaging with social media and homeschooling your children in the 21st century is one way to "opt out." Most people cannot and will not do that, but I would highly recommend it.

These men and women are Nazis, Fascists, Communists, Satanists, Elitists, Eugenicists, Neoliberalists and straight up evil. These criminals have infiltrated every government agency in the world through blackmail, pedophilia, criminal financing, bribery, secret organizations, and mafia tactics. They have designed all governments to operate as corporate entities and chartered subsidiaries of their corporate houses and monarchies. They are mass human traffickers, mass murderers, drug and weapon kingpins, and war criminals who should burn in hell for their crimes against humanity.

I wrote this book to expose the powerful elite groups of the 21st century. I am aware there are many secret societies and probably too many to name and add, but for this book I focused solely on the groups that are in complete control on the world stage in the 21st century. The real power. I wanted to write a book breaking down the power structure for people who want a deeper understanding of how the world works and to gain an understanding of how we got here. I wrote this book for anyone who has ever been called a conspiracy theorist. I wrote this book for anyone who has been called crazy. You are not crazy, and neither am I.

CONTENTS

SYNARCHY **10**

THE BLACK NOBILITY **31**

13^(TH) HOLY MEROVINGIAN **62**

THE GREAT WHITE BROTHERHOOD **71**

ZIONISTS **77**

JESUITS **90**

VATICAN **99**

BILDERBERG GROUP **106**

CLUB OF ROME **111**

COMMITTEE OF 300 **116**

COUNCIL ON FOREIGN RELATIONS **122**

TRILATERAL COMMISSION **129**

ROYAL INSTITUTE OF INTERNATIONAL AFFAIRS **133**

FEDERAL RESERVE **140**

TAVISTOCK **148**

WORLD ECONOMIC FORUM **161**

PHI BETA KAPPA **167**

CHAPTER ONE: SYNARCHY

"There may be nothing scarier than the synarchist enemies of the United States."

Do you question the world around you? Do you internally feel something is wrong, but you can't figure out what it is? If you had the choice to know the actual truth, would you really want to know? As humans, there are many questions we ask ourselves. What does it mean to be human? Why do we exist? What happens when we die? Are we alone? To me these are the most puzzling, tormenting and ominous questions we as humans are faced with in life.

Although we can theorize and speculate all day, deep down, we know these questions will never be answered. And maybe they are not meant to be answered. But why do we keep searching? If you are anything like me or if you purchased this book you are probably asking yourself the same questions. Why do politicians never get anything done? Why are there so many wars? Why are there so many false flags? Why is human trafficking a thing? Why are pedophiles protected? Why are there so many homeless people? Why are there so many diseases? Why are there no cures available? Why are the roads, airports, schools, transportation so terrible? Why is there so much evil? Who controls the world?

Living on earth is faced with many challenges but I am part of the resistance. Since I was a child, I always knew there was something just not right with the world. Seeking the truth and having this obsession to understand it brought me to discovering the secret societies of the world. Once I discovered these hidden groups, I was able to connect the dots and make sense of this upside-down world I am living in. The harsh truth is that psychopaths run the world. These people feed off of negative energy and chaos. They are the personification of evil. Who are they? What are they?

Synarchism (synarchy) means "joint rule". The word is derived from the Greek stems syn meaning "with" or "together" and archy meaning "rule". In the conspiracy theorist world, the word synarchy is used to describe the shadow government or the deep state, a form of government where political power rests with a secret elite and hidden from the public.

A deep state is a type of governance made up of secret and unauthorized networks of power operating independently from the official government (political) leadership in pursuit of their own agenda and goals. Deep state organizations operate in opposition to the agenda of elected officials by obstructing, resisting and subverting their policies, conditions and directives. The deep state will work tirelessly to overthrow a sitting politician or use tactics like blackmail to achieve their sinister goals. Throughout history all major countries have their own networks of deep state puppets. The big power countries with deep states of their own are Turkey, Russia, Israel, Egypt, Germany, Iran, Pakistan, Lebanon and China. Some of these people are either Jesuit trained (Manchurian candidates), blackmailed, or (possibly) cloned. Let's talk about human cloning for a moment.

You can't talk about human cloning without talking about Donald Marshall. Donald came on the scene around 2011 with his infamous Facebook post about the celebrity cloning centers. Donald Marshall claimed that the cloning centers are run by the G20, an international group of state leaders and central banks and the current chair is Guiseppe Conte, some ex Italian banker most likely connected to the Black Nobility. He claimed that celebrities sell their soul by getting killed and cloned. He claims every "A-list" celebrity is involved.

Donald claimed that it was his face on the Megadeath album "The World Needs a Hero" and it honestly looks like him. He claimed that photo was taken right after his clone was tortured and murdered at the cloning center.

What's even crazier is that the Megadeath album released in 2019, a new remastered version of the album shows the skeleton and no image of the dead man. Why is that?

Donald claims that he remembers attending these secret meetings when he was child starting around five years old. He claimed that he was sold to the "program" by his parents who were in the illuminati. Marshall says he had no understanding of the top-secret technology known as R.E.M.-Driven Consciousness Transfer which is used to transfer one's consciousness during the natural R.E.M. cycle of sleep into an identical clone located at the cloning center many miles away.

Marshall explains that when he goes to bed at night, his consciousness is stolen while he sleeps and is held hostage until his real body wakes up. He maintains that this consciousness transfer happens almost every night, even though his real body never leaves the room. Once his real body wakes up his clone body drops limp. Marshall claims that this transfer can only take place once the brain has fully entered R.E.M. sleep cycle. Once you begin to dream, they can steal your consciousness and take you wherever they want you to go.

Donald Marshall claims that top-secret experiments in human cloning have been conducted for decades in deep underground military bases (DUMBS) all over the world. He claims he has seen human cloning first-hand and that these top-secret cloning techniques can be done in many ways. He says the clones are "near perfect" to the original person and can be used as stand-ins for top government leaders and elected officials or sent on spy missions or for dangerous acts of espionage.

The reason why the public never sees any of this is because all cloning activity happens deep underground on government property with highly restricted access. Marshall claims there are thousands of cloning bases underground which were built at strategic points all over the world and the public has no idea what goes on down there. Marshall remembers visiting the secret military bases as a child even though he didn't realize he was a clone at the time. He recalled seeing clones suspended in glass tubes, suspended in water. He said the place smelled of urine and the "grow rooms" are dark and dirty. He claims it takes a little over five months for the clone to full grow and reach completion.

Donald Marshall claims there are many ways to create clones. In *repetition cloning*, scientists can create ideal conditions in the lab for the new life to grow, resulting in a baby clone. He says this process is extremely time consuming as the baby needs to develop like a normal human baby. In *duplication cloning*, the genes are manipulated by mutations and clones can be grown to full maturity in a matter of months and used immediately. Donald has claimed that the 2005 moving, The Island, is exactly what is happening now. A group of wealthy elites invest millions of dollars to care and feed their clones who live on this isolated compound, unaware that they are in fact, clones. The sole purpose is for organ harvesting. Organ harvesting happens to be a real thing in the world of human trafficking. Marshall claims that human cloning is deeply flawed, and clones have serious side effects like unpredictable behavior and little impulse control.

In order to fully understand how this happened it is necessary to revisit the Postwar events in Germany, following the end of WW1, when Hitler was named the leader of the Nazi party. One thing you may not know about Hitler is that he believed in the Vril-ya. While serving time in Landsberg prison for treason he read Bulwer-Lytton's 1871 novel *The Power of the Coming Race*. This book was about a master race who called themselves the Vril who claimed to be descendants of ancient Atlantis. The Vril had an unlimited source of energy. Once Hitler became the Chancellor of Germany, he sent teams of people into caves and mines all over Europe searching for the Vril. He made expeditions to Asia and worked with the Tibetan lamas who knew their way around the caves and mines. Once this Nazi-Tibetan alliance was formed, the lamas shared their knowledge of the indigenous race of lizards living deep underground.

At the time, these Vril lizards knew all of the locations of abandoned military bases dating all the way back to Atlantis. These bases were filled with aircraft, technology and weaponry deep within Antarctica. The lizards had no use for the technology but were willing to trade the Nazi's for something else. The Nazi's obtained the Atlantean technology and sold out the human race. After all, the David Bowie song, "The Man Who Sold the World" was allegedly about Adolf Hilter.

Marshall claims that the Vril lizards have been interacting with humans long before the Nazis came around. He says that for centuries the royal families (Black Nobility) have had a secret pact with the malevolent lizards. The Black Nobility received valuable resources buried deep within the planet, such as gold, minerals and gems in exchange for the secrecy of the existence of the Vril and as long as they were provided with a steady supply of humans to consume. Now this all sounds pretty wacky! Think about all of the people that go "missing" in the world? Why are there so many missing people? Why have there been so many whistleblowers coming out about these deep underground military bases? Why do they all end up dead?

In the book, *The Dulce Wars* by Branton he claims that the Grey aliens have been manipulating human DNA and have practiced human cloning for a long time. The grey alien narrative was popularized by Betty and Barney Hill who claimed they were abducted in the 1960's. The "grand deception" is described as a grey alien/lizard/illuminati alliance where any opposition to the New World Order will create a conflict to reduce the population of the planet, followed by a rapid series of shocking events, earthquakes, worldwide stock market crash, while putting everyone in the world under mind control that could last 3-7 years but will end in an American victory, aided by a divine alien intervention. WTF?

The first whistleblower of the Dulce base was American Businessman Paul Bennewitz and he claimed there was an extensive UFO base at Dulce where aliens were controlling people with electromagnetic devices. We also had Phil Schneider and Bill Cooper who both wrote books, shared lectures of their experience and unfortunately died under mysterious circumstances. What is going on underground? Are these men crazy? Are they mind controlled? Are they telling the truth?

Deception is the biggest element to these psychopath's success. The ability to deceive the public is their master tool. Knowledge is power. Their lies diminish the knowledge of your ordinary citizen which makes life confusing. What is really amazing is their ability to create many different kinds of agents to program the masses. In the programming a variety of things are used from colors to catchphrases to agent provocateurs.

A sleeper agent is the idea of placing someone somewhere in society while they live a normal life for years without ever being used. This is by design. This provides a legitimate smokescreen for what they are all about. It is façade. It is fake. These are your typical mind-controlled slaves. The concept of mind-controlled slaves is no secret anymore. The CIA has publicly admitted to their tactics from projects to **MKULTRA, PROJECT BLUEBIRD, PROJECT ARTICHOKE,** and **PROJECT MONARCH**. Other related projects were **PROJECT MKNAOMI** and **PROJECT MKDELTA**. These programs were illegal using drugs, hypnosis, electroshock therapy, sensory deprivation, isolation, verbal and sexual abuse and other forms of mind control and torture.

Back when journalism actually existed there were many articles and books written about the similarities between government sex scandals, human trafficking and elite sex slavery. And they all related to mind control, blackmail or both. Through the Freedom of Information act we have learned about Operation Paperclip, which brought more than 1000 German scientists to America after WW2, to continue mind control experiments in the United States. This was approved in 1946 by President Harry Truman. Out of **OPERATION PAPERCIP** came **PROJECT OPERATION MIDNIGHT CLIMAX**, which subjected innocent people to high doses of LSD without their knowledge. And these projects eventually transformed into PROJECT MKDELTA which involved the mixture interrogation and drugs. Stanford University and Harvard led the psychedelic drug experiments and pushed LSD to Timothy Leary, Allen Ginsberg and Ken Kesey. Ken Kesey wrote One Flew Over the Cuckoo's Nest and organized the hippie community known as the Merry Pranksters, who traveled America, hosting LSD parties and it was all funded by the CIA.

Robert Hunter, poet and lyricist for the Grateful Dead, was a student at Stanford was paid to take LSD, mushrooms and mescaline. Boston mobster "Whitey" Bulgar said he was subjected to weekly injections of LSD while serving time in the Atlanta prison in 1957. Lawrence Teeter, the attorney for Sirhan Sirhan, believed that he was operating under MKULTRA mind control techniques when he killed Robert F Kennedy. Ted Kaczynski, the Unabomber, said he participated in a 200-hour mind control experiment while attending Harvard. Kaczynski described it as brutal. Post-MKULTRA, Kaczynski suffered from gender dysphoria and contemplated having gender reassignment surgery. After he was arrested, he went on to write books about technological slavery and the decline of civilization.

PROJECT MONARCH was named after the monarch butterfly and it is something you are born into, no exceptions. The Monarch butterfly passes trauma knowledge through genetics to their offspring, from generation to generation. Trauma memory and the ability to dissociate are the key components to creating a sex slave. Dissociation was first discovered by American Indian Tribes who would participate in trauma ritual dances while hunting. In India they would force children to sleep on beds of nails or walk on hot coals. And the children of Buddhist Yogis were taught to dissociate into a hypnotic trance. In reality, all of these practices are deeply rooted in occultism and rebranded to the West as the new age movement. The Illuminati families and aristocracy otherwise known as the Black Nobility, visited these groups to master these practices on a mission to do two things: create a master race and to take over the world through complete and total mind control. Otherwise known as the New World Order.

PROJECT MONARCH training begins in infancy or early childhood. The children are sexually abused, electroshocked and tortured until their minds shatter, creating amnesiac barriers that creates new personalities, called alters, in which they are told are butterflies. At 18 months of age, the child is tested to determine if they can dissociate enough to be selected for the program. The child must learn to match identical items, even before they can speak. This is so they will start to build mirrored images in their mind. Broken mirror images are a symbol or indicator that the victim's mind has shattered, and they are a part of this elite program.

The standard age for sexual grooming in boys is three. This programming typically begins by receiving oral sex. Females go through "charm school" where they are taught to dress sexy and learn the act of seduction. They are taught how to walk, talk, look at men, use their eyes and how to please men in different ways. If you wonder why there is so much grandpa porn available, it is for this reason. The CIA and MI6 use retired programmers and abusers to train young slaves and they film it. A lot of the porn industry is CIA conducted mind control experiments.

Children of the Illuminati are taught to *NOT BREAK THE CIRCLE*. A black mat with a white circle is spread on the floor. The child is taught to stay within the white circle. If they leave the circle, they are subject to torture that could go on for hours or days, to teach them obedience. If they obey, they are rewarded with food or water. If they complain that they are bored or cold, they are subjected to punishment. As the child gets older, ritual trauma starts. The parents might choose to traumatize them on a specific holiday, particularly their birthday, because that is far more damaging. And when their birthday comes around the following year, they are put back into the memory of abuse.

Harmonics and sound waves are used to manipulate human neuron pathways to the subconscious. The brain has four types of brain waves, alpha, beta, delta and theta; and PROJECT MONARCH has a program for each brain type. Alpha is agenda-based programming. You might see victims portraying the Illuminati symbols or tattoos. Beta is sexual programming. Delta is specific programming for assassins, special agents or soldiers. Theta is psychic programming. Tracking and ID implants or microchips created by IBM have been implemented and perfected in these victims.

John Gittinger was a Navy Lieutenant during WW2 and specialized in evaluating personalities. He joined MK ULTRA in the 1950's but went on to work for PROJECT MONARCH. He developed the Personality Assessment System (PAS) to evaluate and predict human behavior in a child. The test is divided into three dimensions I = Internalizer, F = Flexible and A = Adaptive. This assessment could predict whether a child would become a computer programmer, entertainer, assassin or other CIA asset. If a young boy was overly aggressive, he would be marked for war monger or future general. If a girl could sing, dance or has charisma she would be marked for the entertainment industry. These designated roles within the Illuminati are known as "SPINS". The CIA works closely with the Tavistock Institute to create social movements and lead culture where they see fit. These roles are dominated by politicians, athletes, performers, evangelists and TV journalists.

Jim Morrison, David Crosby, Frank Zappa and John Phillips were all children of high-ranking members of the American Military and lived in the neighborhood of Laurel Canyon, a one-time home to the Air Force's Photographic Group. Jared Leto, actor and cult leader, lives in the Hollywood Hills military base today. The Group's mission was to defuse the antiwar movement by getting kids hooked on rock music and drugs. Woodstock was only made possible because Nelson Rockefeller, the Governor of NY, approved and helped fund it. It was just another mind controlled psychological operation to push cultural change.

There is no doubt in my mind Jim Morrison was a PROJECT MONARCH victim. His dad, Captain George Stephen Morrison, was responsible for initiating the Gulf of Tonkin incident, a false flag to get the United States engaged in the Vietnam War. Jim Morrison's alter egos were named the Lizard King and Mr. Mojo Rising, all sexual in nature. In the Doors song, *The End*, Jim sings about wanting to have sex with his mother before he commits suicide. He once said of the song, "Sometimes life is too painful to tolerate. I was saying goodbye to my childhood. Life hurts more than death." But why would we sing about fornicating with his mom? Incest seems to be a major theme associate with PROJECT MONARCH.

The most sought-after Father for these breeding programs is the pedophile father, particularly fathers that molest their infant babies. The CIA knows that if a father would abuse his own daughter the man has no conscience. This type of man could go on to program other children with no regret or remorse.

Cathy Obrien, a PROJECT MONARCH whistleblower, claims her father abused her from infancy and all of her siblings. Her older brother went on to rape her during her youth. She grew up in Muskegon, Michigan which she called "Pedophile capital". When her father got caught distributing child pornography, he was propositioned to sell his kids into the monarch program, which he did. Her father was offered a deal by President Gerald Ford and Cathy was prostituted out to Canadian Prime Minister Pierre Trudeau, Michigan's state senator Guy Vanderjat, Gerald Ford himself, and West Virginia Senator Robert Byrd (who eventually became her owner and handler).

Listen to what Cathy said about the Jesuits: "I'm not saying everyone who is Catholic is bad, but there is a criminal faction within the Catholic church, who call themselves the Jesuits, which is the intelligence arm of the Vatican." Cathy stated that much of her abuse was done at Bohemian Grove, where cocaine and baby sacrifice was rampant. At one of the ceremonies, her vagina was mutilated and carved to resemble an evil face. Cathy says it is for the visual pleasure of the sadistic abuser. In Cathy's book, "Transformation of America" Cathy said the first time she met Hilary Clinton she was forced to strip naked and show Hilary her mutilated vagina. Hillary was so turned on she screamed "GOD!" and performed oral sex on Cathy. Hillary then yelled "Eat me, oh god, eat me now!"

Brice Taylor, another PROJECT MONARCH whistleblower, came out with a bombshell book called "Thanks for the memories". The pdf is free online for anyone to read. She said that all monarch slaves tattoo themselves and you will find many of them have butterflies. She also made bold claims that Sylvester Stallone filmed dolphin porn with the sex slaves along with other bestiality films. Brice Taylor mentioned in her book that her mother would take her to sex slave auctions for Illuminati families that appeared to be children's fashion shows.

Peter Pan and Tinkerbelle programming is a mind control script for never growing up. If you Google "Michael Jackson Art" it's pretty obvious to know he was subjected to Peter Pan programming. In 2020, Paris Hilton made explosive accusations against the boarding school, Provo Canyon, she attended as a teenager, claiming she was verbally, sexually and physically abused, which left her with insomnia, anxiety and trust issues. She claimed she was kidnapped from her home and sent to the boarding school while she saw her parents in the dark hallway as they did nothing to stop it. After she spent a year at the school, she emerged as the Paris Hilton we all know today. She was obsessed with Disney and named her dog, Tinkerbelle. She can be seen wearing Disney princess costumes from the last two decades.

In the movie *The Butterfly Effect*, the cast plays a group of young adults who were psychologically traumatized as children, being coerced by one of the neighborhood parents to take part in child pornography. This leads the main character to have blackouts and amnesia, which is a sign of Beta Programming. Beta programming is the ultimate sex slave program. Cat alters come out at this level known as kitten programming. Abusers of this programming are known to wear red shoes and say, "Purr for me kitten" which will activate the beta slave alter. Clothing with feline prints denotes kitten programming and you can see it everywhere in Hollywood.

Alice in Wonderland programming is mostly used. The white rabbit is a programming figure who will seduce you into seeking adventure through inaccessible information. The rabbit represents the master. The white rabbit is an important figure to the slave. As you can see, many celebrities like to dress up as Alice or use Alice in Wonderland themes. Other major symbols of monarch programming are castles, flowers, bird cages, and hourglasses. Cathy Obrien claimed that Dick Cheney kept an hourglass as a reminder that "the sand that sifts through the hourglass is a measure of your worthiness to live or die."

NXVIUM, the sex trafficking cult, led by Keith Raniere and actress Allison Mack branded their cult members with their own initials. The founders of this sex cult were Nancy and Lauren Salzman, Clare Bronfman (daughter of Edgar Bronfman and friend to Jeffrey Epstein) and Kathy Russell (Russell of the 13 bloodlines). Nancy Salzman was a psychiatric nurse who was trained in hypnotism and Neuro-linguistic programming. It has been revealed through declassified documents these techniques were used to program mind control victims in PROJECT MK ULTRA. What's even more disturbing, Nancy Salzman and her daughter Lauren were slave masters, recruiting women and tasked with locking them in dark rooms for years. This type of trauma splits the mind and causes dissociation. A very twisted mother/daughter duo. All five of the founding members were indicted on federal crimes as of 2019. Mind control themes are everywhere.

One of the most intriguing MK ULTRA stories is about former fashion model, Candy Jones. Jones eventually started recalling morbid memories of being sexually abused by her parents and shared memories of being locked in dark rooms, not being able to socialize with children and having her fingers smashed in a nutmeg grater. As a result of the abuse, she developed an imaginary friend, Arlene. She grew up to participate in beauty pageants and modeling, a likely career path for these mind control victims.

Later in life, due to Candy's bizarre behavior, her husband had her participate in hypnotherapy. During these sessions in the 1960's she revealed she was groomed by the CIA and military with torture and painful sadomasochistic sex. She said she participated in sexual blackmail and delivered messages for the CIA. Candy Jones is the first MKULTRA sex slave victim to go on record, which we now recognize as PROJECT MONARCH. PROJECT MONARCH was not declassified through the government but was revealed through a series of books by whistleblowers.

In PROJECT MONARCH, there are two people assigned to one slave, which they call handlers. If either handler were to die, this would activate the slave's suicide program. If the handler loses control of the victim, internal voodoo will carry out a spell to get the alters in check and to obey.

Using voodoo on a slave is called "Layering." And this brings in the demonic and satanic connection.

PROJECT MONARCH is heavily tied in with Satanism. This isn't about whether satanism or the satanic panic is real, but the fact is, satanism is a tool used to traumatize children. Satanic imagery is used to traumatize the masses. Thanks to Wikileaks we started to see the curtain open and reveal the dark nature of some of these rituals the elite partake in. Spirit cooking is a popular one. Spirit cooking is the act of taking blood from the tongue or genitals, mixed with semen to attract certain demons. These sacrifices can be a family member, friend or first-born child. These rituals force the slaves to take oaths, sign blood contracts and make blood covenants. These sacrifices can be a family member, friend or their first-born child. This is to reinforce the trauma, solidify the layering of demons in the programming and the act of selling one's soul.

These blood signature's go in what the Illuminati calls the "Great White Book" and if they break the oath or covenant, their signature will change color and they will lose their power. According to Cisco Wheeler, "All United States presidents are forced to sign this great white book and are threatened with death if they fall out of line. All United States presidents are born within the same bloodline which make them perfect contenders for mind control." Cisco was asked what happens if a president doesn't fall in line? And she said, "look what happened to Kennedy."

Growing up, monarch slaves are repeatedly told that God is cruel and judgmental. They are read bible verses that tell of God's wrath and God's anger. By the age of 5, the monarch slave is given hypnotic drugs, and the demons have been ritually placed inside the child. By age 12, they are told about their genealogical history and introduced to their demons who they call spirit guides. PROJECT MONARCH sex slaves are subjected to trances and demonic possessions. Demons come with a price and that price is blood. According to high level demonology, certain powerful spirits can be manipulated through blood sacrifices. All of the chakra points and orifices on the human body can serve as portals. A high influx of demonic energy is accompanied by a burning sensation.

The term "Hidden Observer" is a generational demonic entity that works with the programmer and the child. The demon is asked a series of questions to find out what the child's biggest fears are. Most people are born with specific fears: snakes, blood, spiders, or water. The hidden observer will tell the programmer which fear will work best for the programming, because the demonic entity never lies to the master. Demonic entities are why Tarot and psychic readings are so accurate. These messages are truth but are coming from the forbidden tree of knowledge. The programmer, the demon and the child's creative mind work together to create alters or multiple personalities. When you understand mind control and the main principle behind the Illuminati, it is very simple. Get everyone mad at God and you can get them to commit any sin. Get everyone mad at God and they lose hope. Great effort is taken by the illuminati to keep people pissed off and in a state of constant fear or paranoia.

These disinformation agents of influence can be under mind control or ideologically motivated to use their status and power to sway the minds of the public. After all, the media controls the masses. These agents are people on the news, journalists, professors, Hollywood actors and politicians. There are agents whose job it is just to confuse people by disseminating legit information. Contract killers are used by the mafia as rogue agents to do a particular hit job with no connections. Deep cover agents are programmed multiples (people with dissociative identity disorder who suffered from **PROJECT MONARCH**) who can be triggered and activated at any time by their handler to carry out a specific duty or sexual espionage.

Notional agents are fictitious agents who are created with a real identity to mislead but are not who they appear to be. Jeffrey Epstein would be a perfect example of a notional agent. Spoon-feeder agents are used to build up a person's credentials over the years but fail to provide any real or new information. They might put out already known secrets mixed with disinformation once they gain respectability. In reality, there are very few people trying to expose the New World Order. Legitimate whistleblowers tend to end up dead. The power of mind control tactics goes deep and by now it is a perfected art for these psychos.

Another tactic these people have used are monopolies. The elite love monopolies. Their trick is they find a good product or business model everyone wants, and they eliminate all of the competition by either destroying them or buying them out. In other words, here are your corporations! Walmart has killed small business. When you put the concept of "monopoly" on the world stage you can now see how they do it with religion, banking (controlling finance), media and government.

There are numerous Illuminati neighborhoods, homes, restaurants, breweries, schools, colleges and other institutions carrying out the standard practice of public trickery, in other words, they are an illusion. They are not what they seem. Their public persona could be "squeaky clean" but behind the curtain they are pure filth and trash. A good example of this would be the Disney company. Walt Disney worked very hard at maintaining a perfect image for himself and his company. We know now that many victims of trauma-based mind control were secretly programmed at Disney. "When you Wish Upon a Star" is a popular programming song. Not one company has sold witchcraft as successfully as Disney. Every movie introduces occult themes, cannibalism and sexual subliminal messaging.

Disneyland and Disneyworld are a main source of pride for America, but it is important to know that they are programming centers. These places create mind-controlled slaves. These places provide a place for rituals, porn and other satanic activities. When you go back in history and see all of the famous people who have come out of Disney and the problems that follow them it is easy to see the pattern. Why are there famous politicians and kings visiting Disney? Because it is a sinister place with illuminati slaves. The goal was to create a place for people from all over the world to visit, with no suspicion. They have been masters at creating such a place.

Steven Rockefeller and Walt Disney traveled and spent time together with Dr. Hadley Cantril, an expert on human behavior. Walt Disney's property in Florida was totally controlled under Disney's jurisdiction. The property has its own laws, their own police force, their own hospitals and their own tax rate. No outside authority can interfere with Disney. This is how Disneyworld became its own crime syndicate. Mind controlled victims have come forward about the underground tunnels and bases at Disneyworld.

Disney is all about the "BREAD AND CIRCUS" and this concept goes all the way back to the time of the Roman Empire. Going all the way back to the oligarchical leadership who have been in control for centuries know all about the bread and circus. If the masses are provided with food and entertainment, they are easier to control. This is why the television is our worst enemy. Most people just watch television and don't even realize they are being programmed.

Have you ever noticed how many Disney stars have suffered from drugs, suicide, sexual abuse or found themselves involved in porn? This is not an accident. These kids were sold and passed around sexually from the time they were children. Most were born into PROJECT MONARCH and groomed through the Hollywood system. I wish everyone would boycott Disney and everything associated with it. Sadly, Disney is engrained in American culture.

In 2009, Courtney Love posted this on Facebook: "Britney's dad molested her. Imagine the father that molested you owning you for slavery while you're forced to sing songs picked for their sexual content every night. Insane right?" Britney started her career with Disney and was under management by pedophile Lou Pearlman. In Lynne Spear's memoir, Through the Storm, she casually detailed how Britney would sacrifice chickens in the backyard, as if it were normal. And in 2006, Britney shaved her head, drew a 666 on her forehead saying she was the antichrist and screamed that she wanted everyone to stop touching her. People have become privy to Britney's bizarre Instagram posts and conservatorship with her father. The hashtag #freeBritney has drawn attention to is story.

Lindsay Lohan started her career as a Disney kid and suffered a drug fueled life with abuse and crazy parents. She had bisexual relationships with Paris Hilton, Britney Spears and Samantha Ronson in the 2000s, was part of the "anti-pantie party" where no one wore underwear and the paparazzi constantly photographed their privates as they hopped out of their limousines and cars. Like other Disney stars, Lindsay hung out with creepy pedophile photographer, Terry Richardson and spent nights at clubs coked out of her mind with her mom, Dina. There was a leaked photo of what looked like Lindsay and her mother French kissing. These people have problems.

It was also alleged that Brittany Murphy had an incestuous relationship with her mother, and it was up to Brittany to support her financially. It was rumored that Brittany, her husband Simon and Brittany's mother all slept in the same bed together before they died. Brittany was a known escort and yachter. Most Hollywood actresses do not make a living acting. You must do a deep dive into the world of yachting. Actresses and models are flown all over the world to meet with rich and powerful men in exchange for sex. This is how they financially support themselves.

Heather Locklear was born into a Disney family. Her mother was a Disney Executive and her abuser. Heather married Richie Sambora of Bon Jovi and had a daughter, Ava. They got divorced when Sambora allegedly learned of the incestual relationship Heather started with her daughter when she was only 4. It was rumored Heather was sleeping with Charlie Sheen and to please Sheen, Locklear would include 4-year-old Ava in their sex sessions. It was around the same time Denise Richards filed for divorce from Charlie after discovering child porn on his computer. Richie Sambora and Denise Richards started dating right after their divorces. Perhaps they had a sad and tragic event that brought them together. Heather was awarded joint custody after a devastating battle with Sambora but was arrested for choking her mother thereafter.

Doing a quick Google search of celebrities wearing "Disney ears" or celebrities obsessed with Disney makes it easy to see which celebs are victims of PROJECT MONARCH. It is no coincidence these men and women were groomed from childhood to become stars due to their bloodline and generational satanic incestual abuse. John Phillips, the founder of the band, the Mamas and the Papas, was another satanic generational mind-controlled victim. His alter ego was named "Papa John" and he was the son of a high-ranking US Marine of WW1. His daughter, Mackenzie Phillips, started her career with Disney and found fame on the 70's show, One day at a time. By age 11, she was addicted to cocaine and alcohol, both introduced to her by her dad. When she was 19, she woke up from a blackout, and was having sex with papa John. The incestual relationship went on for ten years. The incest ended when she became pregnant and had an abortion.

Drew Barrymore was born into the famous Barrymore acting family in the 1970's. Her godfather is Steven Spielberg. Before we go farther into Drew's creepy past, let's talk about Spielberg for a second. In 2013, actor Crispin Glover released an essay called '*What is it*'. He wanted the reader to ponder why focused Spielberg's movies were generally centered around young kids and mentioned Michael Jackson, that they could possibly shar the same love for little boys. Spielberg's adopted daughter, Mikala, spoke out about her childhood sexual abuse. She said she was surrounded by predators, groomed and abused her whole childhood. Mikala is now a porn star, suffered from alcoholism and eating disorders. Mikala is now married to someone thirty years her senior.

Drew Barrymore (Disney star) said she got drunk for the first time when she was only eight years old and did drugs with her parents. Drew and her mother used to frequent studio 54, snorting cocaine and watched adults having sex. When Drew was 14, her mother went to rehab, Drew emancipated from her parents and moved in with David Crosby. She went on to pose nude for Interview magazine at the age of 16, playboy and has been married three times.

Nickelodeon is another cesspool of pedophiles ironically having to do with children programming. Jamie Lynn Spears, Britney Spears' younger sister was a Nickelodeon actress and close with pedophile TV producer Dan Schneider. She got pregnant when she was 15 and rumors circulated that the baby really belonged to Dan. Dan is infamous for having a foot fetish and making his child star minions suck their own toes and make sexual jokes about feet on television.

Amanda Bynes, another Disney and Nickelodeon child star, accused her father of sexually abusing her when she was young and adding "he should be in jail". Like Britney, Amanda has a strange conservatorship with her father. She suffered from public meltdowns, drug problems, eating disorders and became famous for crazy Twitter rants which ultimately got her kicked off. She sent a letter to her lawyer and cryptically capitalized certain letters of the email and it spelled out "DAN DID IT". This was a reference to Dan Schneider.

Hillary Hawkins, former Nickelodeon child actor, released the *Molestation Monologues* saying they are based on true stories. Ariana Grande, former Nickelodeon child actor, was notoriously exploited on the show Victorious, talking about "being wet" all the time and putting her own toes in her mouth to appease Dan's foot fetish. Jennette McCurdy, former Nickelodeon child actor, created a YouTube channel where she shared her own personal videos. One video is titled "He Touched Me" and wrote in the description that it is "autobiographical". She posed a video titled "Dan Schneider" where she looks distraught, hair a mess, crazy makeup and screams, "look what you've done to me."

Dan Schneider recently deleted over 4200 tweets regarding children and his foot fetish. You can see them all online through various threads. Very disturbing. But it wasn't just him at Nickelodeon who were into kids. Ezel Channel, Marty Weiss and Brian Peck were all arrested at different times in their career.

And then when we thought it couldn't get any weirder, Disney child actor, Orlando Brown accused Will Smith of raping him and that Michael Jackson set the whole thing up! And of course, we've all seen the weird incest videos of Will Smith kissing his son on the lips. Macauley Culkin, another Disney child actor, started a band called "The Pizza Underground". All of their songs are super weird and just have images of pizza. Was he hinting at something? Corey Feldman and Elijah Wood have addressed Hollywood's pedophilia problem.

Cody and Dylan Sprouse were child actors on Nickelodeon. Cole Sprouse became infamous for his cryptic Twitter posts alleging to the boy's trouble past in the industry. He once posted about having to perform oral sex to older men, but it was removed and now completely scrubbed from the internet. What I find to be strange is Cole was accused of sexual assault out of nowhere. Could this have been a message to him? The twins were forced to dress as girls on Disney and in movies. What kind of psychological damage does this do? Hollywood has been trying to emasculate men for years.

I find it really disturbing and sad that many child actors that have been pumped through the Disney or Nickelodeon machine end up with severely complicated and unstable lives filled with pornography, drugs, suicide or murder. From Wikileaks emails to music videos to movies the pizza themes are all too bizarre. Pizzagate may sound crazy to most but there are things that need to be investigated. There is an underground pedophilia problem in the world and too many people died trying to expose it.

Understanding how mind control works is the first step to combatting this psychological warfare we are dealing with. Learning about propaganda is another way to fight it. Why do people believe propaganda? Here are a few reasons why: 1) Social pressure 2) Our emotions are targeted 3) People have short attention spans 4) (Some) people are cognitively lazy 5) confirmation bias all the way and 6) Repetition – the more we hear these narratives repeat, the more likely people will start to believe it. You could also call this conditioning. I've had moments of weakness where I've started to question even my own beliefs; this is the mind game. They want everyone confused.

This control over the media translates to control over the people. The powerful elite understand how important it is to keep everyone dumbed down, fat and distracted. They don't want critical thinkers in their society because anyone who is taking the time to critically think will wake up from their programming.

By now it is easy to see patterns in world events, read between the lines of fake news stories and call out the despicable actions of our corrupt leaders. They are all working together using the same playbook and I believe there has never been a time in history where we, the people can turn it all around. I do not believe these people are as smart as they think they are, and I believe their plan in unravelling. And although there are compliant people who wear the mask to work in attempts to avoid confrontation. I do believe the silent majority would fight for their life if tyranny literally came knocking at their door. And I know a lot of us are armed, they have yet to take our guns away, but they sure have tried.

There are very few groups that fall under **The Round Table**. These groups include the Bilderberg Group, The Club of Rome, The Committee of 300, The Royal Institute of International Affairs, the Trilateral Commission and the United Nations. The Round Table organization was conjured up by Cecil Rhodes, a gold and diamond magnate and politician. Cecil Rhodes believed that white people were the "first race in the world" and was a white supremacist. He believed that white people should remain the supreme race and he mercilessly manipulated South Africa and took the land away from the native black people. He played the African tribes against each other and started wars in order for them to destroy each other. Divide and conquer is one important technique of the Illuminati.

THE ROUND TABLE
- COUNCIL ON FOREIGN RELATIONS
- TRILATERAL COMMISSION
- UNITED NATIONS
- ROYAL INSTITUTE OF INTERNATIONAL AFFAIRS
- BILDERBERG GROUP
- CLUB OF ROME

Rhodes wanted to develop an American elite of philosopher-kings who would have the United States rejoin the British Empire. Rhodes said the goal of the Round Table was to create a World Government controlled by the British Illuminati. He believed in the New World Order and was the front man for the Round Table. The House of Rothschild banking dynasty are the true controllers of these groups. The Rothschild family owns every single central bank in the entire world, except for Cuba, Iran and North Korea.

The Round Table organizations are a key part to the day-to-day manipulation of the military, banking, business and politics. These men create the problems and offer the solutions. In his last will, Rhodes provided his wealth for the establishment of the Rhodes Scholarship. The Rhodes Scholarship is an international post-graduate award for students to study at the University of Oxford. Notable Rhodes Scholars are Bill Clinton, Rachel Maddow, Ronan Farrow, Pete Buttigieg, Susan Rice, Bobby Jindal, Kris Kristofferson and numerous Prime Ministers and Presidents of countries.

Frank Aydelotte wrote in his book *American Rhodes Scholarships*, "In his first will Rhodes states his aim still more specifically: the extension of British rule throughout the world, (with English as the world language), the foundation of so great a power as to hereafter render wars impossible and promote the interest of humanity. 'The 'Confession of Faith' (part of the testament) enlarges upon these ideas. The model for this proposed secret society was the Society of Jesus (Jesuits), though he mentions also the Masons."

Adam Weishaupt founded the Bavarian Illuminati on May 1, 1776 for the purpose to control the world. Weishaupt's role as the Illuminati founder has long been recognized as models for the Communist methodology. Weishaupt also used the structure of the Society of Jesus (Jesuits) and re-wrote the code in Masonic (Freemason) terms. Rhodes' secret society was organized on the conspiratorial pattern of circles within circles within the Illuminati. The Round Table was organized for Lord Rothschild and run by Lord Alfred Milner. These men worked behind the scenes to create WW1. This was only the beginning. Every war since has been orchestrated by these groups to bring the change necessary for their world domination.

2020-2021 is a different kind of war. It is an information war, a psychological operation of the highest level. They have not only attacked America and world with a "virus", but they have infiltrated world governments with their Communist agents through blackmail and espionage. They have rigged every presidential election since after John F. Kennedy. The 2020 election was rigged and used to gaslight the country to spring us into either a revolution or civil war. I am writing this book in January of 2021 so we will have to see what happens. The looming Great Reset seems like it is a train that isn't stopping.

It is important to realize the existence of these groups, to get a grasp on how the world operates and why there is so much confusion and chaos. From politics to social media to garbage Netflix, they want us dumbed down and distracted on every level. If you can overcome their temptations to give in and strive to live a somewhat free and healthy life (mentally and physically), you have won. Delete your social media. Get involved on a local level. Turn off the news. Don't fall for the daily psychological operation. They want your mind. These powerful groups oversee the entire world, they control the money and the people. They are the trillionaires. They are the One Percent. And at the very top, lies the Black Nobility.

THE BLACK NOBILITY

> *"The legendary dragon has two wings, right and left. The real war is between the Christian based constitutional republic of America and the Luciferian cult based socialist empire of Bavaria. But do not be fooled! The right and left -wing movements are Machiavellian, created by the Black Nobility!"*

What is the Black Nobility?

The Black Nobility's roots can be traced back to the Venetian oligarchs of Khazar, or otherwise known as the Khazarians. These Khazarians married into the roman royal houses in the early part of the 12th century. After the Khazarian victory over the Arabs, the future emperor, Constantine the 5th married a Khazar princess and their son became Emperor Leo the fourth also known as Leo the Khazar.

The Black Nobility are traditionally defined as Roman aristocratic families who overthrew the Pope and the papal states and took over any nobles who were in allegiance to the pope. Before the rise of the Roman Empire and their dominant power, existed a very specific cartel of oligarchal families, mainly in Persia, Greece, Babylon and Phoenicia. Over a period of time, there were successions and newly emerging empires due to the Medes and Persians who were conquered by the Greeks. And the Greeks were conquered by the Romans. And it was this period of time which resulted in a lot of marriages between different oligarchical families, bloodlines and empires leading to the expansion of this ancestry that eventually settled in Venice, known as the Black Nobility.

The first of three crusades in the Middle East and the capturing of Jerusalem from the Muslims around the year 1123 established the power base of families living in the republic of Venice. During this time, they captured significant trading routes through Syria, Israel and the Arabian Peninsula. The Venetians were able to develop and provide military support for the crusaders into the middle east; and this is how Venice became an economic trading powerhouse.

The Venetian oligarchs believed they had the right to rule. They believed they were born to rule as an elite while the rest of the population would be condemned to slavery and oppression. One thing that the majority of oligarchs believe were the writings and teachings of Aristotle. Aristotle claimed that slavery is necessary because some are born to rule, and others are born to be ruled. The venetian oligarchs were known to use tactics such as controlling money and looting. "Divide and Conquer" was their mantra and everything they touched turned into war. Their essence can be summed up with the word Empire. They identify as a master race while everyone else are identified as slaves.

They were known for creating chaos and breaking down civilizations. These families gained power and influence strictly due to trading rights of goods, their ability to dominate human affairs, depressions, wars, famine, and plagues. Especially the black plague and the thirty years war, which both have links to Venetian intelligence. The Venetian Intelligence assisted Genghis Khan while he attacked and wiped-out powers that resisted the Venetian bankers. The Venetian oligarchy transferred many of the family assets to northern Europe which created the emergence of the Bank of England, which became the leading bank of the eighteenth century. The Venetians were responsible for convincing their ally Edward the third of England to wage war with France which became the Hundred Years War. This war threw France into chaos before Joan of Arc defeated the English. Joan of Arc was born from a peasant family but was canonized as a Catholic Saint. Joan of Arc was known to cross dress. She would wear men's military clothing to avoid being raped because the uniforms were so hard to get on and off. Cross dressing in the middle ages was a capital crime, meaning repeated charges could end in the death penalty. Joan of Arc was executed by burning.

The Venetians really came to power when they married into the House of Guelph. The Guelphs supported and backed William the third, from the House of Orange as he took over the throne of England. This victory over England resulted in the creation of the Bank of England and the East India Company, which have ruled the world since the 17th century. The

East India Company was an international drug trade trafficking mainly opium.

These operations were eventually transferred to London and it is London who controls and owns the United States. Washington DC, London and Vatican City are in essence Catholic establishments under international maritime law. They all have the same Egyptian monolith, the obelisk, which symbolizes the sun god "RA". The Black Nobility believes that Ra is the sun, with his unblinking all-seeing eye he will enlighten and illuminate.

The royal family of England, the Windsor's, descend from the House of Guelph of England. The Guelphs are also intertwined with the German House of Hanover. Another close Black Nobility family in England are the Grosvenor's. This family still owns at least 300 acres of land and Grosvenor Square in London is owned by the family and it is where the American Embassy is located.

The House of Hapsburg of Austria is another Black Nobility family that remains in power today. Karl Von Hapsburg is currently the leader and he is the son of Otto Von Hapsburg who was one of the strategic drivers of the European Union. The key objectives of the European Union included keeping Russia out of Europe and keeping Europe a Catholic superstate. The Odescalchi's are considered to be one of the top Black Nobility families on Earth and have command over CERN. Their ancestry traces back to Cernobio, Italy which is where the name derives. Fabiola Gianotti is the current Roman director and if you study the logo you can see three sixes, which is the number of Satan. Tom Cruise married Katie Holmes at the Odescalchi Castle in Italy. The great granddaughters of Mussolini still run the Order of the Roman Aquila which is the Roman military.

These families earned the title of "Black" nobility from their ruthless lack of morality. They are untraditionally described for employing murder, rape, kidnapping, assassination, robbery, and all manner of deceit on a grand scale, operating with no hesitation to attaining their objectives and worldly agendas and goals. These families all have immense wealth. And money is power. The most powerful of the Black Nobility families are located in Italy, Germany, Switzerland, Britain, Holland and Greece.

In the beginning these families moved to Rome to serve as a benefit to connect with the Vatican. Many of the members of Black Nobility families also became high-ranking clergy of the Vatican and even Popes. The Black Nobility papal families that have gone extinct are: Aldobrandini, Savelli, Caetani, Farnese and Conti.

The house of Savoy, a Black Nobility family, was established in the year 1003 and this family grew in power from ruling a few countries in the alpine region such as France, Switzerland and Monaco to becoming the absolute rule of the Kingdom of Sicily in the 1700's. The Savoy family entered Rome in 1870 and overthrew the pope and the papal states and took over. This marked the end of a thirteen-hundred-year rule of papal Rome. At the time the pope was seen as both the spiritual and political leader of not just Rome but much of Europe. And because of this takeover, Italy and Rome would be under the control of a secular political government. This is how people like Mussolini was able to reign as a fascist leader for so long.

After this takeover happened, the pope confined himself to Vatican City and claimed to be a prisoner in the Vatican. He avoided the appearance of accepting the authority of the new Italian government and state. Since then, the Black Nobility has been in control of the Vatican and the Holy See ever since. The Holy See also called the See of Rome, is the jurisdiction of the Pope. The Holy See is the jurisdiction of the Catholic Church and international law, which governs Vatican City.

There are two kinds of laws that rule the world. The first is civil law. This is the law of the land. The second law is Uniform Commercial Code otherwise known as the UCC. This is the law of God in the world of business. It doesn't matter what country you live in; you and your business are working under the UCC. The UCC is based directly on Canon Law which is the law of the Catholic Church. Canon law is a system of laws and legal principles created by the Catholic Church to enforce specific behaviors and actions of individuals. The people who enforce these laws are members of the Roman Catholic church, so these people are Bishops, popes, Priests, deacons, etc. Those who are versed and skilled in canon law, and professors of canon law, are called canonists. Canonist is just a fancy term for lawyer. Lawyers who understand canon law. The word "canon" comes from the Greek word Kanon, which means measuring stick or in other words the rule or norm.

Fast forward to 1929 and you have the Lateran Treaty which established a truce between the Italian government and the Vatican. This treaty basically made the Vatican exempt from taxes and gave Black Nobility family members dual citizenship in Italy and Vatican City. Many of the Black Nobility houses have died out but the houses that still exist are Colonna, Massimo, Orsini, Ruspoli, Pallavicini, Theodoli, Sacchetti, Borghese, Odescalchi, and Boncompagni-Ludovisi.

The Black Nobility families believe they have a divine right to rule and when Queen Victoria, the matriarch of the Venetian Black Guelphs, died in 1901, the Black Nobility believed that in order to gain world-wide control it would be necessary for the members to go into business with non-aristocratic leaders of corporate business on a global scale. And in the 1900s the doors to ultimate power and selling out were opened to what the Black Nobility referred to as "the commoners."

This decision by the Black Nobility led to commercial marriages between old Black Nobility families of Venice and Genoa with the Anglo-American financial juggernauts. These Anglo-American powerhouses included The Bushes, the Morgan's, the Goldman's, the Lehman's, the Sachs, Schroders, The Rockefellers and the Rothschilds.

The union of the Black Nobility with American families led to the establishment of the international drug trade which began with the East India Company, the parent company of the Committee of 300 and international espionage that was birthed at the bank of England. And it is these families that have spawned, intermarried and work closely with the Russian mafia, the Sicilian mafia, The American Italian mafia, The Armenian mafia, Israeli Mafia, Greek Mafia, Royal family of Iran, Royal family of Afghanistan, the Vatican, the Jesuits, Chinese Triad Gangs, Hollywood, Albanian mafia, the British Monarch, Scottish nobility, Spanish Nobility, French Gangs, Knights of Malta, South American Drug cartels and more.

These powerful and wealthy groups all work together to remain in total control, to stay powerful and wealthy. The network has grown tremendously since the early 1900s. If you really want to break down how they have so much money and power, it comes from dominating raw materials, such as gold, copper, zinc, lead, and tin. It is no accident that London is where most of the commodity exchanges happen. These Black Nobility families have their tentacles in every secret or private organization in the world. The Club of Rome, United Nations, Bilderberg Group, Trilateral Commission, Committee of 300, Council on Foreign Relations, Tavistock, and more.

The Black Nobility predates the illuminati and Freemasonry by many hundreds of years. The alliance of freemasonry and the illuminati was created in the 1782 congress of Wilhemsbad only to further expand the influence of the Black Nobility. There was a mason by the name of Francis DeVirieu, a French nobleman who wrote a book about the French revolution and in that book, he detailed the importance of this meeting with Jesuit Adam Weishaupt and the coming together of these two groups.

When we think of power and wealth you can look no further than the Black Nobility. These families have all the wealth. Trillions. It was the "Cult of Apollo" that created the Roman Empire and enslavement through debt. These traditions have been passed down to the elites that run the world today and they are still using the same methods to brainwash and control the world. And the quickest way into the minds and hearts of the people is through global communication.

The bible once said the devil dwells at Pergamon. Pergamon is now modern-day Turkey. Is it a coincidence that Robert Maxwell, father of Ghislaine Maxwell ran a successful business called "Pergamon Press"? The God of Pergamon, which is still worshipped today as a live serpent, and is the snake god of medicine, Asclepius. The rod of Asclepius is now the logo for modern medicine used by all health physicians called the caduceus. In the Book of Numbers, God told Moses to erect the bronze serpent rod from Asclepius to protect the Israelites who could die from fiery serpents. The son of Apollo is the Illuminati's term for "Antichrist". Who is the son of Apollo? It is Asclepius. Who is his mother? Her name was Coronis. It is important to note that in Greek mythology Asclepius became so good at healing he surpassed both Chiron and his father, Apollo, and was able to evade death and bring others back to life. This caused an influx of human beings and Zeus resorted to killing him to maintain balance in the numbers of the human population. Interesting that the Illuminati's version of the antichrist is a "healer of humans". So, who is the real antichrist according to Christians? Some would argue the pope. Some would argue members of the Black Nobility. Time will tell.

It is the Black Nobility who practice human sacrifice and perform black mass rituals. The black mass ritual was invented by Catherine de Medici and practiced in the court of Louis XIV, the French nobility Catholic King. The members of mass wear talisman, which are necklaces that are thought to hold magical powers through the children of demons. Asmodeu, was one of Lucifer's followers and one of the seven princes of hell. In the classification of demons, this is where we get the seven deadly sins. Each prince of hell represents one of the deadly sins. And it is the children of these princes of Hell who are worshipped at these Black Nobility rituals. In both the Holy Bible and Jewish Bible, these princes are referred to as "false Gods." The Black Nobility calls these deities, "EL" where the word "Elite" derives.

Martin van Meytens, a Dutch painter for the Black Nobility, painted *Kneeling Nun Recto* in 1731. Its home is the museum in Stockholm, Sweden in the permanent exhibit "Lust and Vice." A picture is worth 1000 words.

It is important to note that the white supremacist groups are working with black supremacist groups on the world stage. Any kind of power struggle within is just a conquer and divide tactic to dumb down the masses. White versus black, man versus women, gay versus straight versus pansexual, etc. One group that you may not have heard about is the Five Percent Nation. The Five Percent Nation work under the Black Nobility and the **Royal House of Khan.**

The Five Percent Nation or the Nation of Gods and Earths (NOGE) is an Islamic and Black Supremacist organization involved in organized crime, murder, gang stalking, and terrorism. It was founded in 1964 by Clarence Edward Smith who was a member of the Nation of Islam. The NOGE teaches that black people are the original people of planet Earth, and therefore they are the fathers (Gods) and mothers (Earths) of civilization.

The NOGE teaches Supreme Mathematics, which is a fancy name for numerology, and the Supreme Alphabet, which is a set of principles used to understand humanity's relationship to the universe. The NOGE does not believe in a God but instead teaches that the "Asiatic Blackman" is God, and his proper name is "Allah", the Arabic word for "God". Members of this group call themselves Allah's Five Percenters, which reflects the concept that ten percent of the people in the world know the truth of existence, and the elites and their agents keep eighty-five percent of the world in ignorance and under their controlling thumb; and it is the remaining five percent who know the truth and are determined to enlighten the eighty-five percent. In the song Raw Hide by Ol' Dirty Bastard, Method Man raps the following lyrics, "wicked women putting period blood in stew, I fear for the eighty-five who don't have a clue."

Black male students are taught they are Gods and the astral twin of the Sun. In Supreme Mathematics, the Black man is symbolized as "knowledge." The Black women are taught they are symbolic of planet Earth because women produce and preserve human existence. The women are referred to as "wisdom." The Five Percent Nation do not consider themselves a religion because they do not worship any deity other than themselves. They believe they are the highest power in the known universe. Clarence Edward Smith developed a curriculum of eight lessons that includes Supreme Alphabets and Mathematics. The Five Percent Nation are required to master each lesson and are expected to "think and reason by forming profound relationships between the lessons and significant experiences in life."

Hip Hop was infiltrated by the five percent movement to coin terms like "ciphers", "dropping science" and to influence everyone around the world. According to their teachings, the Cipher is 360 degrees of the completion of knowledge (120 degrees), wisdom (120 degrees) and understanding (120 degrees). To have all of these means that the cycle is constantly spinning and there is no room for negativity to enter. These artists include AZ, Big Daddy Kane, Brand Nubian, Common, DJ Khaled, Erykah Badu, Ghostface Killah, LL Cool J, Jay Electronica, Jay-Z, Khalid, Nas, Papoose, Poor Righteous Teachers, Raekwan, RZA, Wiz Khalifa, World's Famous Supreme Team and Wu-Tang.

Wiz Khalifa takes his stage name from the Arabic word Khalifa which means "successor". The name pays homage to the **House of Khalifa**, the current ruling family of Bahrain, who are Sunni Islam. Sunni Islam is the largest denomination of the Islam religion. Wiz is short for wizard and their sorcery is mind control. LL Cool J is a member and goes by the name Lord Supreme Shalik. In the song Life's a Bitch by Nas, rapper AZ rapped, "We were beginners in the hood as Five Percenters, but something must've got in us, cause all of us turned to sinners."

Erykah Badu is tattooed with Nation of God regalia and defended Hitler in many interviews. Adolf Hitler was allied with the Muslims during WWII. Rudolf von Sebottendorf was one of the founders of Nazi ideology, a Freemason, Sufi occultist (Islamic Mysticism) and founder of the Thule society. Jay Electronica signed to Jay-Z's Roc-Nation and in a song, they collaborated together, Jay-Z raps, "I'm ready to chase Yakub back into the caves; These are the last days, but do I seem fazed?" The Yakub refers to the "creator of white people.

The Nation of Islam teach that Yakub (the biblical and Qur'anic Jacob) from the Tribe of Shabazz, created the white race on the Greek island of Patmos. The Nation of Islam believe that Yakub established a secret eugenics policy by killing all of the dark babies at birth. The process of creating the white man took over 600 years. Malcom X believed he was a descendant of the Tribe of Shabazz and even used the surname Shabazz after 1949. Tim Russert once asked Farrakhan if he believed white people were "blue eyed devils" and he responded, "in the book of revelation, it talks about the fall of Babylon. It says Babylon is fallen because she has become inhabited with devils. We believe Babylon is America."

Jay-Z wearing the Five Percent Chain

The lyrics in the song Lucifer by Jay-Z say, "Lucifer, son of the morning! I'm gonna chase you out of Earth. I'm from the murder capital, where we murder for capital." Khepri is a scarab-faced god in ancient Egyptian religion represents the morning sun. The scarab is a dung beetle which feasts on the dung of other species and can ejaculate semen into a dung ball which creates life. Eating excrement is practiced by sun worshippers and Satanists.

Jay Electronica had an affair with Kate Rothschild and lived in London for a while where he was trained by the Knights Templar in witchcraft and mind control. The Rothschilds intermarried with the Aldobrandini family of Black Nobility (Rome). The surname Aldobrandini derives from the Arabic word "Aldebaran" which means "the bright one of the follower", because it follows the Pleiades star cluster. The Aldobrandini's have Arabic ancestry from the Moorish Invasion. The Arab royal families were known for sex trafficking of European and African women. Arab and Berber pirates kidnapped these women and sold them in Africa and the Middle East. When the Moors invaded Europe, they were involved in sex trafficking of women as a continuation of the Arab slave trade.

Pope Benedict XVI Papal Coat of Arms

Pope Benedict XVI was good friends with King Abdullah of Saudi Arabia, and they have been photographed holding hands. The **House of Saud** are Sunni Muslims like the Muslim Brotherhood and they basically share the exact ideologies of imposing their religious Sharia law as state law. The Black Nobility of Rome, Rothschilds, and House of Saud are all working together and directing and financing various secret societies, organized crime, and supremacist groups. The link between all of these groups is occultism and satanism.

The **House of Mansour** family are Egyptian billionaires, and all three brothers went to school in the United States. There is no one to investigate the Arab billionaire royals who rule their own nations and that is why they are used for money laundering and making these criminal payoffs. In the early 1980's a man by the name of Khalid Al-Mansour was the principal advisor to Prince Alaweed Bin Talal of Saudi Arabia. Alaweed is a member of the Saudi Arabia royal family and was listed in Time magazine as one of the top 100 most influential people of 2008. Coincidentally, the same year Barack Obama became President of the United States.

Khalid Al-Mansour sought after a man named Percy Sutton, who had been one of the mayoral candidates of Manhattan in 1977 and the lawyer of Malcolm X. Sutton claimed that he was asked by Khalid Al-Mansour to write a support letter to Harvard for Barack Obama. When Sutton asked why, he replied, "I am raising money for Obama's education. Top members of the Royal Saudi family are looking to exert influence in the United States.

In 1979 an article titled, "Will Arabs Back Ties to Blacks with Cash?" was written by a Chicago reporter by the name of Vernon Jarrett. Vernon Jarrett was the father-in-law of Valerie Jarrett who later served as the senior advisor to Barack Obama. Her father-in-law, Vernon, was rumored to be best friends with none other than Frank Marshall Davis, a former Chicago journalist, communist and poet. Frank Marshall Davis moved to Hawaii and befriended Obama's mother, Ann, when Barack was just 10 years old. Davis was known to have taken an active role as mentoring Barack until he was 18, around the same time Khalid Al-Mansour was seeking the money. Barack Obama was knighted by the House of Saud and frequently used drones for targeted killings of Shia Muslims and enemies of the House of Saud in Yemen. Barack Obama implied he has Muslim faith and arguably the worst president America has ever seen.

The Khan royal family of Iran claims to be descendants of the ancient Fatimid and Ismaili dynasties (descendants of prophet Muhammad) and are top managers of the Five Percent Nation. They have close connections with the Black Nobility of Italy and are related to the Irish-Anglo Guinness family known for their brewing, banking and politics. The Khan family currently resides in Switzerland. Aga Khan IV, who is the current leader of the Nizari Ismaili's (Assassins), was born into British nobility and his father had an affair with American actress Rita Hayworth. The ancient Order of the Assassins were an Ismaili society that practiced witchcraft and specialized in murder. This is where we get the word assassin today.

"Hash" which is condensed marijuana resin derives from Hashashins who would drug people before assassinating them. Aga Khan and his family are the descendants of this ancient order. In 1959, while visiting the Los Alamos laboratory in New Mexico, Aga Khan was gifted with Trinitite, residue from the first nuclear bomb detonation. Why would a Royal Prince be gifted this from Los Alamos?

Aga Khan with Trinitite at Los Alamos Laboratory, 1959.

Aga Khan was the first Muslim to receive the honor of Knight Grand Cross of the Order of Merit of the Italian Republic. This group is heavily involved in money laundering, criminal financing and terrorism. They are involved in satanic sexual ritual abuse and mind control and they specifically target white people.

Tony Khan and his father, Shahid Khan own the Jacksonville Jaguars and All Elite Wrestling (AEW). Shahid Khan was featured on the front cover of FORBES magazine as the richest person in America of Pakistani origin. This is no coincidence; they are descendants of the Royal House of Khan. This ancestry could also go back as far as Genghis Khan.

The Nation of Islam was founded in Detroit, Michigan by Wallace Fard Muhammad in 1930. The Dearborn Mosque in Michigan is run by the Muslim Brotherhood and using proxy groups that have been promoting Sharia law in the United States. Louis Farrakhan took over the Nation of Islam's headquarters in Chicago in 1977. Farrakhan has strongly encouraged members to study Dianetics and undergo Scientology auditing. Louis Farrakhan once said, "the only way white folks can come out of this because you cannot be reformed you cannot reform a devil, you have to kill the devil. If someone offered me what Brother Jay Electronica was offered by Brother Jay-Z, I too would accept it with the biggest smile on my face, for I too, as all of us in The Nation of Islam, are The Five Percent."

Other famous Muslims are Dave Chappelle, Mike Tyson, Muhammed Ali, Chaka Khan, Dr. Oz, Kareem Abdul-Jabbar, Ice Cube, Hakeem Olajuwon, Shaquille O'Neal, Lupe Fiasco, Bella and Gigi Hadid, Cat Stevens, Jermaine Jackson, Busta Rhymes, Akon, Mos Def, French Montana, Snoop Dogg and Professor Griff.

Black Nobility families that operate currently are as follows…

The **House of Pallavicini** are top members of international banking, owners of the Armenian mafia, the Lucchese crime family and are related to the Iranian royals. The Aga Khan family of Iran royalty are the heads of Nizari Ismaailisim and have close ties to the Vatican and Italy. You can trace the Pallavicini's to the Bush family particularly George H.W. and his son, George W. The Bush family are directly related to the Von Dem Bussche family of Germany. They were all interconnected in regard to the War on Iraq. Iran and Iraq have been at odds ever since Iraq banned the Jesuits from the country after they established colleges to use as "infiltration." It is alleged that the Armenian mafia is headquartered in Hollywood working under the Russian mafia.

House of Pallavicini Coat of Arms (double headed eagle)

The American mafia is massive. The Gambino's are the most dominant mafia in the United States because they use violence and force to control others. These men are allegedly owned by the **House of Gaetani**. The Gambino's were indicted for sex trafficking underage girls. These men use blackmail to intimidate politicians, bankers and businessmen to create "protection." It has been written that the Philly mob is actually part of the Gambino crime syndicate and is dubbed the most powerful mafia on the planet. Prince Roffredo Gaetani is the top owner of the Gotti's and the Philly mob. Prince Roffredo dated Donald Trump's ex-wife, Ivana, for years. Donald Trump's Atlantic City casino was built by the Philly mob and Trump is known for being friends with wise guys and street guys. Trump's longtime lawyer, Roy Cohn, was a lawyer for the Gambino's and had bizarre associations with the boy's town scandal in Omaha. John Elkann a descendant of the Gaetani family is the CEO of Exor which owns Fiat-Chrysler, Ferrari, Economist Group, CNH Industrial and other companies. This family intermarried with the Rothschilds and the Brandolini's.

Gaetani Coat of Arms

The **House of Orsini** allegedly own the Cleveland Crime syndicate and factions of the Israeli mafia. This family intermarried with the Rosenberg family and together they oversee the Rosicrucian order. The Rosicrucian's are alchemists and alchemy is the manipulation of the body and mind. Think cologne or perfume, that is alchemy. The Orsini family works closely with the Merck family who created the Merck Pharmaceutical company. The Merck company created ecstasy (MDMA) in 1912. The Merck family also had a bank which took over the Rothschild bank during WW2. The Cleveland crime family has a close alliance with the Detroit mafia. Paul Rosenberg, Eminem's manager, is part of this crime syndicate. Pepe Orsini of this powerful Roman bloodline is the Grey Pope and king of the Holy Roman Bloodlines. The "Trinity" (Vatican, London, Washington D.C.) falls under the control of these Black Nobility bloodlines and the Jesuits.

House of Orsini Coat of Arms

The **House of Borghese** allegedly owns the Pittsburgh crime family and the Sicilian mafia and part owners of the Vatican. They have been known to launder money through casinos and have intermarried with the Jewish Warburg family and the Aldobrandini family. The Aldobrandini family own the New Jersey mafia and wineries in Long Island. The Italian and Greek mafias have infiltrated the United States especially New York and New Jersey dominating in cocaine smuggling, heroin markets, professional sports rigging, casino rigging and human trafficking.

House of Borghese Coat of Arms

The **Medici** family are owners of certain Italian and Detroit clans, allegedly. They are interconnected with international banks and financial groups such as HSBC and BlackRock. The Medici family has an alliance with the Jewish French Dreyfus family who owns a private bank called Dreyfus & Sohnes Banque in Switzerland. Many of these Italian noble families have banks in Switzerland. There have been four Medici popes and members of royalty including Queens and Nazis. The Medici's married into the Savoy family who originally established the Black Nobility in 1003. The Medici's have a statue of Hermes at their palace in Rome and this is a nod to the Hermetic Order of the Golden Dawn.

House of Medici Coat of Arms

The **Chigi** family allegedly own the Albanian mafia. The Albanian mafia operates out of New York, London and Israel. The Chigi family can be connected Nazi's and Zionists. Their family motto is "it shines on the top" referring to the Illuminati pyramid, the all-seeing eye. The Chigi family once oversaw the Sovereign Military Order of Malta and knighted several high-level Nazis. Under their Pope Alexander VII they established the headquarters of the Equestrian Order of the Holy Sepulchre of Jerusalem to their della Rovere palazzo. The Chigi papal coat of arms has 6 hexagrams on it just like the Zionist symbol.

House of Chigi Coat of Arms

The **Savoy** family allegedly owns the Venetian mafia, Genovese crime family and parts of the Greek mafia. They are also connected to Russian royals and Vladimir Putin through joint ventures in Monte Carlo, Monaco with casinos. The Savoy family intermarried with the Belgian royal family. The Lucchesi family are Venetian nobles and part owners of the Lucchese crime family as well as the Greek and Israeli mafia. The Lucchese family claim ancestry from the Lombard kings and have intermarried with the House of Habsburg and House of Bourbon who have intermarried with the royal family of Luxembourg. Gary Lucchesi is a Hollywood producer and agent of the family. He produced the movie: *Gotti: The Rise and Fall of a Real-Life Mafia Don*. The House of Savoy and Black Nobility used Mussolini to establish the Vatican as a nation and to weaken and persecute their opposition in Italy. The Mussolini family still live in Rome and have married in with Italian nobility.

House of Savoy Coat of Arms

The **Ruspoli** family are owners of the Montreal, Mexican and South American drug cartels, allegedly. The Ruspoli's intermarried with the Matarazzo's of Brazil and have several family members who lived in these countries. They also intermarried with the American billionaire Getty family of Scottish ancestry. Hollywood actress Olivia Wilde was once married to Tau Ruspoli, a member of this noble family. Many members of this family are members of the Constantinian Military Order of Saint George which is overseen by the House of Bourbon. Many members of this family also married into the Romanian House of Dragos.

House of Ruspoli Coat of Arms

The **Colonna** family are part owners of the Vatican and owners of the Knights of Columbus. They descend from the Counts of Tusculum which produced six popes. This family oversees the Colombo crime family and the Chicago outfit, allegedly. The Knights of Columbus are a Vatican military order that specializes in infiltrating police departments and brainwashing officials. It has been written that this family dominates the cocaine industry and has deals with South American cartels.

House of Colonna Coat of Arms

The **Massimo** family are top owners of the Italian mafia, allegedly. The Massimo's have authority over Apollo Global Management which manages more than 240 billion in assets. Tony Ressler is a covert Knight of Malta and Jesuit educated from Georgetown who co-founded Apollo Global Management. Apollo Global Management owns Constellis Holdings which now owns the mercenary company Blackwater. The Massimo's produced two Popes for the Vatican over 1500 years ago and created the Jesuit Massimiliano Massimo Institute in Rome where Mario Draghi the President of the EU central bank was educated. The Massimo's also ran the Jesuit Mondragone college with numerous presidents. It has been written that Prince Fabrizio Massimo is the real head of the Black Nobility. The Massimo's have been presidents for the Jesuit College of Mondragone which specializes in the Jesuit education of the Black Nobility family members. This family also established the Massimiliano Massimo Institute in Rome which is a Jesuit college.

House of Massimo Coat of Arms

The **Sforza** family oversee the Seattle crime family, allegedly. The Sforza coat of arms has a serpent eating a child. The Seattle crime family are known for sex trafficking and owning strip clubs on the West Coast. I believe Bill Gates, Jeff Bezos and the Pelosi family are all agents of the Sforza family. The Sforza family are ancient nobility who once ruled Milan and manipulated the Milan Stock Exchange. Current Italian billionaires are connected with Milan and the Sforza family. Leonardo Del Vecchio acquired Sunglass Hut, Ray-ban and Oakley and is connected to the Sforza family. In the film *Silence of the lambs*, Hannibal Lector's mother's maiden name is Sforza.

House of Sforza Coat of Arms

The **Odescalchi's** are owners of the Serbian mafia, allegedly and are Roman and Hungarian nobility. This family also works with the Israeli mafia and has residences in London. Tom Cruise, who is a top Scientologist was married at the Odescalchi castle to Katie Holmes and was covertly knighted by them. The Odescalchi family oversee CERN in Switzerland. Cernobbio, Italy is where many Jesuit centers resided until they were acquired by the Odescalchi family in the 1770's. Perhaps this is where the name CERN came from. The Odescalchi's intermarried with the Giustiniani's. "Scalchi" means scales and Giustinianis means "justice". We know that the Supreme Court is run by the Jesuits and I believe Supreme Court Justice John Roberts is an agent of this family. John Roberts was also a professor at Jesuit Georgetown, a member of Phi Beta Kappa and was on the Jeffrey Epstein flight log.

House of Odescalchi Coat of Arms

The **Torlonia** family are a top Roman banking authority and are the Vatican's treasurers. Many Torlonia's have management positions at the Vatican as "prince assistants" to the papal throne. This family are part owners of the Bonanno crime family, Pittsburgh crime family, Kansas City crime family and the drug cartels of Mexico, allegedly. The Torlonia's intermarried with the House of Bourbon and Royal family of Luxembourg where private banking is used for money laundering. The Luxembourg royals attend yearly meetings for the International Monetary Fund (IMF). The Torlonia's have had banking business with the Rothschilds for centuries and banking business in Italy. Prince Guillaume of Luxembourg is also an Italian prince of Parma through his grandfather Prince Felix who was from the House of Bourbon-Parma. He is also Jesuit educated from Georgetown.

"The head of everything is God, the Lord of heaven, After Him comes Prince Torlonia, lord of the earth, then comes Prince Torlonia's armed guards, then comes Prince Torlonia's armed guards' dogs, then comes nothing at all. Then comes nothing at all. Then comes nothing at all. Then come the peasants. And that's all." – House of Torlonia

House of Torlonia Coat of Arms

The **House of Saxe-Coburg and Gotha** are one of the biggest royal families in Europe. This clan intermarried with the Habsburgs, Wittelsbach's and are allied with the Vatican. An American family descendant of this clan are the Steinbrenner's of New York who own the New York Yankees. Many Nazi officers and politicians descended from this family. This family along with the Rothschilds helped engineer the birth of the Nazis and WWII which was a financial power move for both houses. This family are a group of white supremacists who support groups like the KKK. This family has Ashkenazi blood and one of the descendants is Samuel Sachs, the co-founder of Goldman Sachs. This family has most of their money in Switzerland and Denmark and have residences all over the world, including Mexico where they pushed Nazi ideology. David Duke the Grand Wizard of the KKK went to Louisiana State University and met Prince Andreas of Saxe-Coburg and Gotha. It was rumored the Prince recruited Duke to be his "top Nazi propagandist".

House of Saxe-Coburg and Gotha Coat of Arms

The **House of Bourbon-Two Sicilies** is run by Prince Carlo and he oversees the New England crime family, Cuban mafia and crime families in Florida. When we get to the top tiers of world power structures, we have the United Nations, the Jesuits and the Vatican. Above them are the Knights of Malta, The Constantinian Order of Saint George and the Royal Order of Saint Francis. If you want to know who oversees these groups, it is Prince Carlo, the current Head of the House of Bourbon. Prince Carlo is the top authority over the Jesuits and Pope Francis. The New Orleans crime family is owned by the French House of Orleans which is under the House of Bourbon.

House of Bourbon-Two Sicilies Coat of Arms

Prince Carlo took over the House of Bourbon in 2008 when his father, Prince Ferdinand, died. Prince Carlo is a descendant of Prince Raniere, the former head of the House of Bourbon. Where have we heard that name before? Keith Raniere the leader of NXIVUM! Prince Carlo's role as head of the House of Bourbon makes him superior over two groups and they are the Sacred Military Constantinian Order of Saint George and the Royal Order of Francis. The Sacred Military Constantinian Order of Saint George is a non-governmental organization (NGO) that was established in 1718 as the sole international Catholic Order alongside the Knights of Malta.

The Knights of Malta and the Sacred Military oversee international law that governs the Vatican otherwise known as the Holy See and has a permanent observer status at the United Nations. All members of the Sacred Military and the Knights of Malta must be descendants of the Black Nobility. This royal order is responsible for choosing the people who hold consultation positions at the Economic and Social Council (ECOSOC) at the United Nations. ECOSOC is all about sustainable development, it is agenda 2030. ECOSOC also ties into the World Economic Forum (WEF), which was founded by Klaus Schwab, a German engineer and economist.

Prince Carlo and family with Donald Trump at Mar-a-Lago

Prince Carlo and Jesuit Pope Francis

The second group that Prince Carlo oversees is the Royal Order of Francis the First which was founded in 1829 as a merit award to members of the Black Nobility for their public service. The Royal Order of Francis the First, is the equivalent of the Order of the Golden Fleece in Spain. John F. Kennedy and Jackie honeymooned in Mexico at the Mexican president's villa and Jackie wrote this poem that reads: "He would find love; he would never find peace. For he must go seeking the Golden Fleece." Out of all the poems Jackie wrote it was this poem that really stuck out to me. Who was the Golden Fleece?

After spending some time researching, I found two strange parallels. The first parallel is a Greek myth about the Golden Fleece of Zeus's holy ram. The Greek myth goes as follows. The two children of King Athamus, Phrixus and Helle, were condemned to be sacrificed by the orders of their stepmother. Zeus, who saw this as an injustice, released his holy ram the golden fleece to save them. The ram flew down and took the children away and continued to travel a long distance with the children. But during the flight, Helle fell from the ram's grip and plummeted into the ocean, to his untimely death. The area of the ocean where Helle fell is known today as Hellespontine and was named after this famous Greek story. This small region of what is now modern-day Turkey is where JFK JR and his wife Carolyn honeymooned. And just like Helle, JFK Jr. fell from flight, into the ocean to his death.

The second connection was when I discovered the Order of the Golden Fleece, which traced me back to the Black Nobility. When I researched who was the Knight of the Golden Fleece was during JFK's presidency, I discovered it was Robert Hugo, the head of the House of Bourbon! Robert Hugo was the ruler of the Jesuits and the Vatican! You can speculate all day who killed Kennedy but in my humble opinion all roads lead to Rome, the Jesuits and the Black Nobility!

We know it was the Club of Rome that played a huge role in the Cuban missile crisis and tried selling the "crisis management" under FEMA to President Kennedy, but Kennedy didn't want FEMA. FEMA stands for Federal Emergency Management Agency. FEMA is an agency under the United States Department of Homeland security. Homeland is a word derived straight out of the communist manifesto. Homeland security was enacted in 2003 as a response to the 9/11 terrorist attacks. FEMA was established officially by President Jimmy Carter and the National Security Council chief who happened to be Zibigniv Brzezinski. He is the father of tv journalist Mika Brzezinski, was a member of the Council on Foreign relations, the Bilderberg group and started the Trilateral Commission with David Rockefeller in 1973. These are three of the most powerful, secretive organizations in the world.

Zbigniew Brzezinski was a big proponent for advising Jimmy Carter to start heavily engaging with China. We know the Rockefellers have had an alliance with China for over a century and it comes as no surprise to me to connect these dots. In 1970, he wrote a book called "Between Two Ages", in which he wrote, and I quote, "The technetronic era involves the gradual appearance of a more controlled society. Such a society would be dominated by an elite, unrestrained by traditional values. Soon it will be possible to assert almost continuous surveillance over every citizen and maintain up-to-date complete files containing even the most personal information about the citizen. These files will be subject to instantaneous retrieval by the authorities." This sounds like a combination of the China Skynet project and social media. And this was written in 1970.

So now let's go back to John F. Kennedy and FEMA and how this all ties into what's happening today. We have to start with the assassination of John F Kennedy. If we go back in history, we know it was the Club of Rome that played a huge role in the Cuban missile crisis and tried selling the "crisis management" under FEMA to President Kennedy. We know that Tavistock agents approached the president trying to explain how crucial FEMA was to be implemented. But Kennedy rejected FEMA he didn't like it and it was the same year Kennedy was murdered. I'm not saying he was murdered because of FEMA but I think it played a big role and this is why.

In 1972, Richard Nixon signed executive order 11490 called "Assigning Emergency Preparedness Functions to Federal Departments and Agencies". 11490 is a list of 23 executive orders that says the government can suspend the constitution for up to five years during a declared national emergency. In this case they will send Congress home for six months. It does not specify what the emergency is, just that the president has to declare it. Then, while Jimmy Carter was president, he gave all regulatory power under these executive orders that Nixon signed, to FEMA. So, Jimmy Carter basically finished what Kennedy never wanted to start.

In 1993, Bill Clinton signed executive order 12852, titled *President's Council on Sustainable Development*. This executive order recognizes the United Nations as the "law of the land" which basically eliminates our constitution during a pandemic. It is also one reason why since 1993 the United Nations has been dictating where our military troops go and where our bases are. This order gave the United Nations the authority to council a sitting president in regard to Agenda 2030. Under the fancy name of sustainable development. And in 1993, no one was really talking about this. Agenda 2030 was not on most people's radar, but this happened almost 30 years ago. Then we had Ronald Reagan sign into law the Stafford Act of 1988 which pushed more power to FEMA. FEMA then created a program which is now law, signed by George H.W. Bush, separating the United States into ten federal regions. This plan would all be done while the constitution is suspended making sure that the United States cannot come back together and the America that we know will seize to exist. Now when I first heard about this, I thought there is no way this could be real. But then I went to the FEMA website and here it is. The ten regions of FEMA.

March 13, 2020, Trump declared the US in a state of emergency. And I'm not saying all of what FEMA does is wrong, they are a disaster relief program they have been responsive after hurricanes, floods, etc. But the point I'm making is there is this underlying agenda behind FEMA working towards agenda 2030 since the 1960s. And we just have to ask ourselves why? We know that Tavistock agents approached the president trying to explain how crucial FEMA was to be implemented but Kennedy rejected it. That same year Kennedy was murdered. Everyone has an opinion on how and why Kennedy died, most believe it was a coup between the mafia and the CIA, alien disclosure, cloning center disclosure, which could all be very true, but I believe it goes back to the Black Nobility, who ultimately oversee the Italian American mafia and the CIA. And once I discovered Prince Carlo of House of Bourbon oversees the Vatican, the United Nations, and the Jesuits, my next question was, who oversees Prince Carlo? It led me to the discovery of the Imperial Cult of Rome and the Great White Brotherhood otherwise known as the ascended masters.

The **Bufalari** family are owners of the Buffalo and Buffalino crime family, allegedly. This family has Roman ties that are several hundred years old. This family is involved in private yachting and human trafficking. It has been written that the Buffalino's operate near Scranton, Pennsylvania where the Jesuit College, University of Scranton is located. Joe Biden is from Scranton and has two honorary degrees from the Jesuit school. Hunter Biden attended Georgetown and served as a Jesuit after college. Terry Pegula owns the Buffalo Bills and Buffalo Sabres and Black River Entertainment (country music industry). Terry is a billionaire from Pennsylvania and was Jesuit educated in Scranton. He used to work under the American Getty family who married into the Ruspoli Black Nobility family. Pegula resides in Boca Raton, Florida which is where the mafia headquarters is, allegedly.

The **Lanza di Scalea** family owns the Lanza crime family of San Francisco, allegedly. The Lanza's would ultimately be under the control of the Gambino's through the infiltration of East Coast senator, Andrew Lanza of New York. Andrew Lanza is Jesuit educated and a former FBI agent. The Lanza family claims to be descendants of the Bavarian Wittlesbach royal family. Remember Sandy Hook? Remember Robbie Parker, the dad who lost his daughter to the shooter was laughing hysterically just seconds before being filmed for CNN? Who was the "shooter"? Adam LANZA. Is Adam Lanza David Hogg? David Hogg's dad is also an FBI agent.

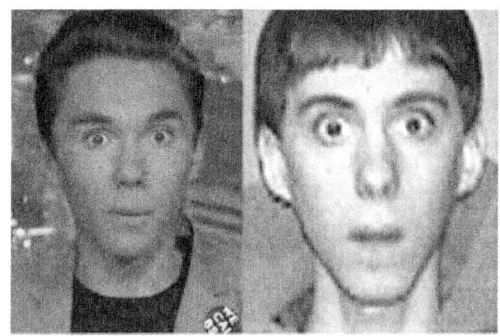

Is David Hogg Adam Lanza?

13TH HOLY MEROVINGIAN

"It is believed that the 13th Holy Merovingian bloodline is where the Antichrist will derive."

The 13th Holy Merovingian bloodline claims to be descendants of Lucifer. These men and women of this bloodline are the European royalty are leaders of the Illuminati and participate in high ranking Masonic and Satanic rituals. According to this bloodline, Lucifer and Christ are brothers. It has been written that descendants of Joseph Smith and other leaders of the Mormon church are both descendants of the Merovingians and are practicing Satanists. The symbols of the Merovingians are the Knights Templar red cross, Arcadia and the Bear, Solomon's Temple, Fleur-de-lis, and King Arthur legends.

Knights Templar *Fleur-de-lis*

It is believed that the Antichrist will come from the 13th bloodline. This bloodline believes they have both the holy blood of Jesus and Satan. Eustace Mullens did extensive research on the Tribe of Dan (descendants of Cain). The Tribe of Dan was prophesied to be the black sheep of the nation of Israel. This tribe's logos were the eagle and the snake, and they ruled the Greeks, the Roman Empire and the Austro-Hungarian Empire among others. It is important to note that this bloodline makes up many of the British, Dutch, German and Scottish monarchies. There are so many branches to this family and numerous secret offspring that these families keep hidden. This bloodline is so extensive its membership branches out to almost all United States presidents including George Washington and George H.W. Bush, Bill Clinton, George W. Bush, etc.

In Gerald Massey's book A Book of Beginning, it describes in great detail how the inhabitants of the British Isles came from Egypt. The Egyptian word "Makhut" means clan or family and became the Irish "Maccu", hence the Maccu of the Donald's" or MacDonald's/McDonalds. The ancient Irish and Scottish people had ties to the Egyptians, Scythians and Greeks. There are many connections between the House of David and Scottish and Irish royalty. The Egyptian god Ptah was changed to Patrick by the Druids and was then Christianized and became St. Patrick's Day. These families are a continuation of the mystery religions of Babylon and Egypt.

The House of Windsor are known to be descendants of the Merovingian bloodline. Prince Charles is related to George Washington, Thomas Jefferson, James Madison, Zachary Taylor, William Henry Harrison, Benjamin Harrison, John Tyler, Harry Truman, John F. Kennedy, Gerald Ford, Lyndon Johnson, the Bush family, Dan Quayle, Barack Obama, Hillary Clinton, Donald Trump. Also related is Robert E. Lee, Winston Churchill and Dick Cheney.

Hillary Clinton is related to Madonna, Celine Dion, Angelina Jolie, Camila Parker-Bowles, Jack Kerouac and Alanis Morrissette. John McCain is the sixth cousin of Laura Bush. Brad Pitt and Obama are distant cousins. Tom Hanks and Mister Rogers are descendants of Abraham Lincoln. Donald Trump and Hillary Clintons 18th great grandparents were the Duke and Duchess of Lancaster, which is the monarch of the United Kingdom, which Queen Elizabeth rules.

When Prince Charles married Princess Diana it was known in occult circles that this was a very important Illuminati union. This marriage was observed and televised like all high-profile occult ceremonies. You can bet any televised marriage is one to be looked into deeper. Do you ever wonder why we are forced to keep hearing about the royal family even though we are in America? It's because they are the co-owners of the country. Princess Diana did not come from the true-blue bloods (13th Holy bloodline), but she was related to a number of illuminati families (Astor, Bundy, DuPont, Amelia Earhart Putnam, Franklin and Teddy Roosevelt). Many rumors speculated that Princess Diana was to marry a Rockefeller, JFK Jr., or Bill Clinton to solidify the tie between Britain and America. There are so many reasons to believe Diana was ritually sacrificed.

Transylvania is in the Transylvania mountains which is the area invaded by the Huns, Mongols and Bulgars. Later it became a battle ground between the Turks, Germans, Romans and Hungarians. The German nobles wrote countless stories of Count Dracula and his blood drinking rituals and described him as a "vampire". Prince Charles is one of the only people alive that is related to Count Dracula via Vladimir IV. The British family have way more power than people can even imagine. They have their tentacles in Australia, the United States and Canada and also oversee British Freemasonry. According to the book *The Unlocked Secret Freemasonry Examined*, Freemasonry, the Illuminati and the Ordo Templi Orientis are all working together behind the scenes to bring in a New World Order and destroy the fabric of society by promoting divorce.

The **Welf** bloodlines (Guelph, Hanovers, Estes) originated from the same clan that ruled Northern Italy and Germany with old French dynasty blood. The House of Hanover are closely related to the House of Este (founder of Este Lauder). The House of Esterhazy are a noble bloodline from Austria/Hungary are and have close ties to the Vatican and the Sovereign Military Order of Malta. The Esterhazy owns the Forchtenstein Castle which is famously known for having torture chambers. The Esterhazy's have shares in the cosmetic company Este Lauder and this company was named after the Houser of Esterhazy which has over twelve billion in assets. If you Google any "Lauder" they are worth billions and most likely serve as ambassadors or high-level positions in the business world. This is no coincidence. Joe Esterhas is a Hollywood screenwriter (Basic Instinct, Showgirls) and his father was a Nazi propagandist. Many members of the noble families have found their way to Hollywood. They are easy to find if you know which names to look for. The Esterhazy's have a number of properties throughout Hungary and Transylvania.

Forchtenstein Castle, House of Esterhazy   *Joe Esterhas*

The **House of Hesse** are a military bloodline that are allied with the House of Habsburg and descended from the House of Brabant. Mayer Amschel Rothschild was the founder of the Rothschild banking dynasty and was employed through William I of Hesse (House of Hesse). The surname Epstein is one of the oldest Ashkenazi Jewish names and derives from the German town of Eppstein, in Hesse, Germany. The Lords of Eppstein are a German Nobility family. The Lords of Eppstein ruled Rodheim vorder Hohe (a district of Hesse, Germany) which is where the true Rodham family name (toponymic evolution) descends from. Hillary Rodham Clinton is one of these descendants. Prince Donatus of Hesse is a top authority over international Nazi's, militaries and mercenaries. It was alleged that he ran the Bush dynasty presidencies through military ops. Prince Donatus is a higher level than the Windsor's and openly flirts with Kate Middleton (wife of Prince William) while William watches. An open secret. Edmond de Rothschild Group uses the Hessian red lion on their bank logo.

The **House of Bussche** family of Germany have close ties with House of Hesse. The true descendants of the Bussche family are the "American Bush/Busch" families. George W. Bush married Laura Walker Bush. The current head of the CIA (Gina Haspel) is actually a Walker. The previous director of DARPA was a Walker (Steven) and worked closely with the CIA. Numerous family members of the Bush family have been Skull and Bonesmen. Skull and Bones is a secret society at Yale University otherwise known as The Order, Order 322 or the Brotherhood of Death. Some notable Skull and Bones members are Prescott Bush, George H.W. Bush,

George W. Bush, John Kerry, Stephen Allen Schwarzman and many other prominent illuminati family members.

George Soros is a puppet but who does he really work for? Soros assisted the Nazis in confiscating property from Jews during his youth. Soros created the Open Society Institute which fund radical political groups as a means to destabilize societies while pretending to represent civil liberties. George Soros who original name was "Schwartz" is from Budapest, Hungary which was ruled by the **House of Habsburg**. The name Schwartz means black. The Schwarzenberg's are co-managers of the Black Monks and the Black Monks manage Bohemian Grove. Bohemian Grove is an all-male secret society of influential politicians and businessmen that make mock human sacrifices to a giant owl (Moloch) and have been exposed for bringing in young male prostitutes to their club. It has also been alleged they have human hunting parties there. Richard Nixon once said, "it is the most faggy goddamned thing you could ever imagine."

The Soros family are agents for the **House of Schwarzenberg**. Prince Karel Schwarzenberg and George Soros have known each other for more than thirty years and support each other's "work". Prince Karel also attends Bilderberg Group and Trilateral Commission meetings annually. It is easy to argue that Austria, where the Schwarzenberg's ruled, is where Nazi ideologies originated from. Adolf Hilter was an Austrian. Gustave Schwarzenegger was an Austrian Nazi and the father of Arnold Schwarzenegger. Arnold Schwarzenegger has been photographed doing the Nazi salute and is a relative to the Schwarzenberg family which is why he has been allowed to become a wealthy and famous Hollywood actor and California politician. He married Maria Shriver (Kennedy bloodline) but is now divorced.

The **House of Bernadotte** has the faggot bundle on their coat of arms. What does this mean? The Fascists are a violent group who run rampant all over the world. The word Fascist derives from the Latin word 'fasces' which means bundle. The word faggot also means bundle. Faggotry is a common male initiation ritual in secret societies. The United States is a federal corporation; it is corporate fascism. Through these symbol they are telling you who runs everything. The faggot bundle can be seen everywhere Knights of Columbus, National Guard flag, the Great Seal of

France and is also found on at least 17 countries and territory flags, globally. The Bernadotte name is connected with Berne, Switzerland and this family oversees Switzerland and Sweden and have intermarried into German nobility. The Wallenberg's are a Swedish family that currently control billions of dollars and the "Wall-Wal" bloodlines are connected. The Walton, Wahlberg, Wallenberg, Wallderdorff families are all connected with Jesuit educated people and corporations in the United States.

House of Bernadotte Coat of Arms (fasces bundle)

The **House of Wittelsbach** are the royal family of Bavaria and were Holy Roman emperors at one time and were granted the title of King of the Romans by the papacy. They were also appointed to be the modern monarchs of Greece under the London Conference of 1832. The German word "wittle" means shine or white. The House of Wittelsbach ruled during the establishment of the Bavarian illuminati in 1776 the same year the United States was established. Adam Weishaupt was born in Bavaria and established the Illuminati under Prince Maximilian II Joseph of Wittelsbach. Marcus Goldman and Samuel Sachs, the founders of Goldman Sachs, are from Bavaria. The Trump family originated from the Kingdom of Bavaria. The Wittelsbach's operate closely and have business ties with the royal families of Belgium and Luxembourg. Levi Strauss was born in the kingdom of Bavaria along with Joseph Ratzinger the ex-pope. The House of Wittelsbach claim to be against the Nazis but are actually involved with many Illuminati members, Jesuits, Zionists and Nazis.

The **House of Stuart** (Stewart) was founded by Robert II who descended from the Kings and Queens of Scotland. The Stuarts produced seven Grand Masters of the Grand Lodge of Scotland. The Stuart family intermarried with the Guinness family who are Irish billionaires, bankers and brewers. This house also intermarried with the House of Wittelsbach, Rothschild, Goldsmith and Guggenheim families. The Stewart family is Roman Catholic and connected to the Order of Malta, Zionists and Vatican knights.

Patrick Stewart and Rod Stewart getting knighted by the British Empire

The **House of Orange-Nassau** are a high-level family that operates as a branch of the Vatican and oversees the Rand Corporation, Koch Industries, Princeton University and BlackRock investment firm. The House of Orange are French Nobility and former Holy Romans that currently rule the Netherlands. The Venetians worshipped Venus and is depicted as the orange planet and the House of Orange have ancestry from the Venetian oligarchs. They have shares in Royal Dutch Shell, Phillips electronics, Dutch airlines and cruise ships. Princeton University's Nassau hall was named after this royal house. Just like the Jesuits, you can find agents of Orange that went to Princeton. John Bogle, founder of the Vanguard group attended Princeton. Eric Schmidt, billionaire and former head of Google, went to Princeton. The Koch brothers originated from the Netherlands and were arguably financed by the Dutch crown.

Prince Bernhard of Lippe-Biesterfeld (Prince of the Netherlands) is the brother of Queen Beatrix of the Netherlands. He belonged to the House of Lippe but was appointed a commander of the Military William Order (House of Orange Order) and awarded with the Knight of the Grand Cross. He is known for founding the Bilderberg group, being friends with Nelson Mandela, Ian Fleming (James Bond author) and David Rockefeller. He was forced to step down after his involvement with the Lockheed scandal. The Dutch royal family are connected to Catholicism, Protestantism, Nazism and the Jesuits.

The College of William and Mary was created by King William III of Orange in 1693 and is a public research university in Williamsburg, Virginia. Next to Harvard it is the second oldest institution in the United States. This is where the fraternity **Phi Beta Kappa** was founded. Notable alumni from this college are George Washington, Thomas Jefferson, James Monroe, John Tyler, Henry Clay, Robert Gates, Patton Oswalt, Jon Stewart, Michelle Wolf, NASA astronaut David Brown, and actress Glenn Close to name a few.

King Willem-Alexander of the Netherlands is the head of the House of Orange-Nassau and is the leader of the Loyal Orange Order of Freemasons. Look at the logo "LOL". There were rumors that this actually means "Lucifer Our Lord". Jokes on us. The House of Orange owns the royal Dutch Shell company. It was the House of Orange that signed the Bank of England into existence.

Loyal Order of Orange (LOL)

There are many other houses and active families that are working together to bring about the New World Order. The Royal House of Khan, House of Saud, Orleans-Braganza, McMahon, Franco, Bonaparte, Isenberg (Eisenberg), Furstenberg, Lippe, Saxe-Coburg, Radziwill, Thyssen, Bussche, Hanover, Douglas, Blumenthal, Rosenberg, Seimens, Merck, Schroder, Stewart, Stuart, Romanov, Bonham-Carter, Seymour, Phillips, Hamilton, Campbell, Murdoch, Sutherland, Astor, Bundy, Collins, DuPont, Freeman, Kennedy, Li, Onassis, Rockefeller, Rothschild, Russell, Van Duyn, Carnegie, Forbes, Getty, Niarchos, Goldsmith, Guggenheim, Oppenheimer, Pritzker, Dreyfus, Sassoon, Bailey, Guinness, Hennessey,

Durst, Romney, Vanderbilt, Steinbrenner, Hilton, Rooney, Hearst, Disney, Cox, Johnson, Zogu, Osman, Khalifa, Khan, Yi, Yamoto, Sihamoni, Khashoggi, Saud, Hashim, Solomon, Mondavi, Dolan, etc.

THE GREAT WHITE BROTHERHOOD

"Welcome to Shamballa."

The Imperial Cult of Rome was the first secret society and the true power behind the Roman Empire. This cult was so top secret and highly classified that even the Roman Senate, governmental officials, and the general public were completely in the dark about who was actually in charge. The cult claimed divine authority to rule through descendance from the lineage of Man, birthed by Minos the Crete, the founder of the Roman Empire. Minos was raised by King Asterion, which translates to Ruler of the Stars. Minos was painted by Michelangelo in *The Last Judgement* painting and can be found at the Sistine Chapel in Vatican City where he is depicted as the devil. According to Greek mythology it's been written that Minos spawned the "master race" popularized by Nazi Germany and currently occupies Switzerland and Greenland as the Great White Brotherhood.

There are two Great White Brotherhoods that control everything in the world; one in Greenland and one in Switzerland. The island of Greenland is officially owned by Denmark, referred to as Greenland of Denmark which becomes the acronym for GOD. In the Holy Bible the allegorical and metaphorical history of the Greco-Roman Empire, the term GOD is a direct reference to Greenland of Denmark. It is also important to point out that the flag of the Holy Roman Empire is identical to the flag of Denmark.

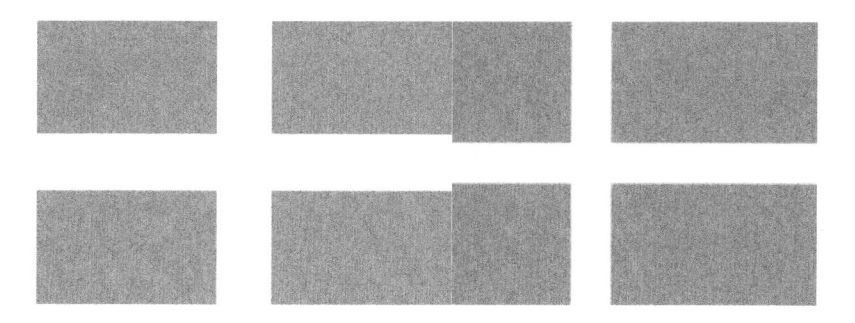

Flag of Holy Roman Empire   *Flag of Denmark*

Helena Blavatsky, founder of the Theosophical society, claimed to receive messages from the ascended masters. Blavatsky was a controversial Russian occultist and philosopher. She gained an international following in the esoteric and Theosophical studies. The Theosophical society named itself after "wisdom of the gods" and emphasized the commonality among all humans. It was her work that inspired the New Age Movement. Blavatsky claimed that Saint Germain was one of the hidden masters of Tibet who secretly controlled the world's destiny.

Many researchers believe that Saint Germain was the son of Francis II of Transylvania. Prince Karl of House of Hesse once wrote that Saint Germain was an alchemist who claimed to have the elixir of Life, the secret formula to immortality (which is what the Rosicrucian's claim to have too). Saint Germain has been believed by many to have reincarnated on Earth as Plato, Proclus, Francis Bacon and numerous others.

Other examples of those believed to be ascended masters are Jesus Christ, Confucius, Gautama Buddha, Mary the Mother of Jesus, Saint Paul of Tarsus (Hilarion), Ashtar Sheren, Sanat Kumara, Archangel Michael, Metatron, Kwan Yi, Kuthumi, Enoch and many others.

Alice A. Bailey claimed to receive numerous revelations from the Great White Brotherhood between 1920-1949. She wrote that the Great White Brotherhood were benevolent spirits aiming towards enlightening humanity. According to Alice A. Bailey Jesus is one of the Masters of the Ancient Wisdom and is the Master of the Sixth Ray. According to Elizabeth Clare Prophet, the Master Jesus incarnated twice as the Emperor of Atlantis once in 33,050 BC and again in 15,000 BC. She said that this was to aid white magicians in the war against the black magicians that was going on in Atlantis at the time. She claims Jesus also incarnated as Joseph of the Coat of many colors in the 17th century and King David (1037 BC).

Guy Ballard, an American mining engineer, studied Theosophy and the occult extensively. Guy claimed that he met Saint Germain at the California mountain Mount Shasta in 1930. This is what he wrote about his meeting Saint Germain that day:

"It came time for lunch, and I sought a mountain spring for clear, cold water. Cup in hand, I bent down to fill it, when an electrical current passed through my body from head to foot.

I looked around, and directly behind me stood a young man who, at first glance, seemed to be someone on a hike like myself. I looked more closely and realized immediately that he was no ordinary person. As this thought passed through my mind, he smiled and addressed me saying:

My Brother, if you will hand me your cup, I will give you a much more refreshing drink than spring water. I obeyed, and instantly the cup was filled with a creamy liquid. Handing it back to me, he said: 'Drink it'."

Guy Ballard went on to write the teaching of the ascended masters via Saint Germain and they are still used today. According to the ascended master teaching, a "master" or "shaman" is a human being who has taken the fifth initiation and is thereby capable of dwelling in the 5th dimension. An ascended master who has taken the sixth initiation (also referred to as ascension) is capable of dwelling in the 6th dimension. Initiation is a concept in Theosophy that there are nine levels of spiritual development that beings who live on Earth can progress upward through. Within these levels there are four basic levels humans can progress through as they reincarnate, and it is believed that evil acts may cause bad karma to cause a soul to regress.

At the fifth level, souls have the opportunity to become members of the Spiritual Hierarchy. This concept was developed by Alice A. Bailey and C.W. Leadbeater in the 1920's. Here are the initiations:

Initiation Zero – The vast majority of ordinary humans live here

First Initiation (Birth to Spiritual Life) – One gains full control of the physical body; they have attained their "I AM" presence

Second Initiation (Baptism) – One gains full control of the astral body

Third Initiation (Transfiguration) – One who gains clairvoyance and clairaudience

Fourth Initiation (Crucifixion) – One who has the ability to remember all past lives

Fifth Initiation (Resurrection) – One can bilocate and levitate

Sixth Initiation (Ascension) – One who can teleport to any place on Earth

Seventh Initiation (Christhood or Avatar) – One who can teleport to anywhere in the solar system

Eighth Initiation (Buddhahood) – One who is completely telepathic

Ninth Initiation (Godhood) – One who comprehends at once all the life on the globe; uses bubbles in space (black holes) to materialize or dematerialize objects and can directly work with cosmic forces outside our solar system (Think Pleiadians)

Tenth Initiation (Planetary Logos) - This being would have had to have been a high-level Planetary Deva in some other solar system before it incarnated inside our planet at the time of the creation of our world

Levels of Initiation Beyond the Tenth – According to Alice A. Bailey, there is a powerful being living inside the sun serving the Solar Logos called the Avatar of Synthesis. Its job is to transmit the seven rays from the heart of the sun through the seven spirits before the throne to all of life in the solar system. This being is called the Ray-O-Light and the only master above all these levels is Christ.

It has been written that The Great White Brotherhood is a racist cult in Greenland and essentially rules the world and likely derived from the Imperial Cult of Rome. The Great White Brotherhood goes by this alias A∴A∴ as well as the Secret Chiefs. Aleister Crowley once confirmed that the A∴A∴ and the Great White Brotherhood were the same entity. The A∴A∴ is a secret spiritual organization written by Aleister Crowley in 1907 and its members are "dedicated to the advancement of humanity by perfection of the individual on every plane through a graded series of universal initiations." American writer L. Sprague de Camp believed that A∴A∴ stood for "Atlantean Adepts."

The Secret Chiefs are a Spiritual Hierarchy which are responsible for the operation and moral caliber of the cosmos. They claim to operate an esoteric organization that manifests itself outwardly into a "magical order" or lodge system. It has been written that they are interdimensional or existing on a different plane. Karl von Eckartshausen believed they met at a special location (Shambala) and are spiritually enlightened beings who lived past incarnations as ordinary humans but have undergone a series of spiritual transformations and initiations. According to the book Sects, Cults and Alternative Religions by David Barrett, he writes that the Great White Brotherhood are a cult of supernatural beings of great power who have risen from the Earth into immortality and watch over the world. The members of this group go by many names: ascended masters, council of light or the esoteric order.

In the book, The People of the Secret, the author states there is a "Hidden Directorate" that has been influencing, guiding and intervening in humanity's destiny over the ages. The Great White Brotherhood claims to have been present in all secret societies and ages and have been in power since the fall of the Roman Empire on Earth. The Great White Brotherhood refers to themselves as man, while other people refer to themselves as human. The term Hue means property of color. These brotherhood men have white skin, red hair and blue or green eyes. In other words, they have the "look of the Irish", hence the idiom "luck of the Irish." The color "Black" consonantly equates down to "B Lack" or "13 Lack", a reference to the 13 bloodlines of the Rome Illuminati which lack black or African blood, hence the term the Great White Brotherhood. Students of the ascended masters teaching believe the world is destined to have a Golden Age (Heaven on Earth) that will be permanent unlike other Golden Ages that came before.

On the flip side if you want to talk about how the Illuminati works today according to modern day occultists, they will tell you the ruler of this sinister empire is Satan. It is known that the Illuminati is Satan's child, and he directs his kingdom every 28 years at a year-long event called the Feast of the Beast. At this event, Satan delivers detailed instructions on how to bring about the New World Order. These instructions are then sent down the chain of command and put into action by the pawns of the evil empire. According to David Hill, "the guiding force behind the Illuminati has always been certain demonic spirits assigned to steer the leaders of the society. These are the demonic rulers and princes who strive to destroy anything pure and righteous. And in the dawning of the new age, these evil entities are appearing as enlightened beings and reptilian aliens."

In the year of 1868, plans for a mock-alien invasion were given at the Illuminati Feast of the Beast and since then secret societies involuntarily accomplices have been pushing this agenda forward since. The aliens working with humans claim to be from different stars, specifically Alcyone in the constellation of the Pleiades. Alice A. Bailey, who knew of Satan's plan for a New World Order wrote quite a lot about the Pleiades in her book *Esoteric Astrology*. Now whether the Theosophical society was working with "demons" or if these entities were real, benevolent ascended masters no one will ever know.

ZIONISTS

"The Zionists indeed learned well from the Nazis."

The top Zionist bloodlines include Rothschild, Warburg, Elkann, Oppenheimer, Walton, Guggenheim, Sassoon, Rosenberg, Lauder, Pritzker, Durst, Fisher, Sackler, Soros, Cohen, and Goldsmith to name a few. These Zionist families are worth trillions altogether and keep their money sealed away in private banks. Zionists are economic supremacists that are mostly involved in white collar crimes including money laundering, criminal financing and human trafficking.

Zionism is a political movement that is run by wealthy Jewish billionaires who seek to monopolize society. This is about Jewish supremacy and control over Jerusalem. The most prominent Jewish family are the Rothschilds. The Rothschilds have been closely involved with the global elite since its inception. The oldest Rothschild went by the name of Uri Feibesch who lived in the early 16th century. His great great great grandson was Moses Bauer who lived in the 18th century and he was connected to Mayer Bauer a rich asset manager in Germany and he acquired all of his wealth during the French Revolution. Mayer Bauer handpicked all the spouses for all of his kids, which came from the global elite families and royals. And this is how the Rothschild banking dynasty started.

James Rothschild made the Parisian house the most powerful bank in Europe because his clients were Napoleon and Ludwig the French rulers at the time. When we look back in history and all the wars from the last three centuries you will start to notice they all ended with a balance of power and the Rothschilds manipulated the wars by controlling the flows of money. And currently the Rothschilds control, Shell, BP, Deutsche Bank, IBM, World Bank Group, International Money Fund, Fed, JP Morgan and a lot of these companies are run by Jesuit educated people.

"I care not what puppet is placed on the throne of England to rule the Empire. The man who controls Britain's money supply controls the British Empire and I control the British money supply." - Nathan Mayer Rothschild

The Rothschilds financed Karl Marx a Jewish Mason and devoted Satanist to write *Das Capital*. Albert Pike and Guiseppe Mazzini who were in strategic positions of power wrote about the plans for communism that were delivered straight from Satan himself at the Feast of the Beast meeting. After creating International Socialism (communism) and establishing National Socialism (Nazism) these ideologies were pushed out through Masonic Lodges and other secret societies in the late 1800's.

Hitler was the offspring of the Rothschild's secret breeding program. Hitler was groomed for his role without even realizing his heritage. It's been written that Hitler learned about his "Jewish bloodline" way after he was in control of Germany. His bloodline is a rare Ashkenazi Jewish bloodline, and it has come to the United States and the antichrist spirit of Hitler lives on. Hitler once said, "I am not only the conqueror but the executor of Marxism!"

The Rothschilds have a majority stake in nearly all the central banks in the world and many of the family members can be seen wearing the red bracelet of Kabbalah which represents anger, fire and holocaust. They currently own De Beers diamond company. De Beers was founded by Cecil Rhodes and was financed by the Rothschilds. The Rothschild family has intermarried with the Hiltons, Goldsmiths, Sassoon's, Aldobrandini's, Brandolini's and Tomassini's and have banking contracts with the Vatican through the House of Torlonia. Baron Jacob Rothschild is a British noble and financier for the British Crown and House of Windsor.

David Mayer de Rothschild oversees the Kabbalah center which is headquartered in Los Angeles and associates himself with many celebrities like Ashton Kutcher, Glenn Close, Kevin Spacey and Sylvester Stallone.

Napoleon Bonaparte was the first political Zionist who proclaimed all the Jews migrate to Jerusalem. The Jesuits and the Black Nobility literally put the Bonaparte's in power and that is why they intermarried with the Italian royal families such as House of Bourbon and Borghese. The Dreyfus family of France have had numerous members knighted under the House of Bonaparte. Julia Louis-Dreyfus is related to the French Nobility swiss bankers notably billionaire Margarita Louis-Dreyfus. This family owns the Louis-Dreyfus Group out of Geneva, Switzerland and is involved in food processing and finance.

Jewish comedians have a monopoly on comedy because they are from Kabbalistic bloodlines. The **Royal Order of the Jesters** is a tax-exempt branch of Freemasonry specifically the Shriners. The Jesters specialize in brainwashing through comedy or clown terrorism (Juggalos). Most major comedians in Hollywood work under the Royal Order of the Jesters. Their motto is "Mirth is King" meaning laughter is king. This royal order was busted in 2008 for human trafficking underage girls, underage sex and drugs. Remember when Jerry Seinfeld and Jimmy Fallon had breakfast on Season Five Episode Eight of Comedians in Cars Getting Coffee? Jerry Seinfeld said, "the best pancakes taste like human flesh." WTF?

The Jesters are run by the German Furstenberg family. Jim Carrey, Kevin James, Adam Sandler, Julia Louis-Dreyfus, Seth MacFarlane, Sarah Silverman, Seth Rogen and Steve Carell are all members (allegedly). The Furstenberg's own Juggalo street gangs. Insane Clown Posse are criminal bosses that run the Juggalo gangs which are involved in assaults, blood drinking and terrorism. They are an FBI official criminal gang. Bozo the clown, remember him? He pays homage to Boso the Elder, a famous German Count.

The Royal Order of the Jesters use comedy for political manipulation and deflecting from serious issues. Barry Diller, husband of Diane von Furstenberg, acquired CollegeHumor.com and is connected to Saturday Night Live, John Oliver, Samantha Bee and the Daily Show. Barry Diller is good friends with Lorne Michaels, the creator of Saturday Night Live. This order was founded in Hawaii and members join by invitation only. Their icon is the Billiken which became popular during the "mind-cure" era which represented a no worry ideal. The Wizard of Oz author, L. Frank Baum, famously kept a Billiken on his piano at home. This group is not really about comedy because most of it is not even funny. They are about psychological warfare.

In 2005, Hillary Clinton attended the roast of Rahm Emanuel. At the end of her speech, she mentioned the word 'Mishpucka', which is Hebrew for the family. The Mishpucka is a term used to describe the Jewish Mafia. In the book, *From Yahweh to Zion*, page 297 states, "The Mishpucka wanted Kennedy dead and turned the operation into a successful assassination, then escaped investigation by hiding behind the CIA's scheme." Susan Lindauer, an antiwar activist, was on the phone with her case worker at the time, Richard Fuiz a Georgetown-educated Psychiatrist and former CIA agent, during the 9/11 attacks. She reported as the planes were hitting the towers, Richard Fuiz screamed in anguish, "The God damn Israeli's!"

In the book *JFK-9/11*, page 193 reads, "Israel has a long history and grand expertise in false flag terror. From the King David hotel bombing of 1946 to the Las Vegas shooting of 2017...What's next?" Do you remember Elizabeth Holmes? She was the founder and CEO of Theranos. She was charged on 11 counts of wire fraud, including defrauding doctors and patients. One of Holmes' board directors was Henry Kissinger. Who was her psychiatrist? Richard Fuiz. He claimed that Holmes was a sociopath, and he knew her since childhood.

In the book, *Bloodlines of the Illuminati*, page 450 states, "The Mishpucka Jewish mafia, Leader Pritzker, lives in seclusion in Libertyville, IL. Pritzker has been active in Chicago for the Mishpuka and for some reason, dead bodies keep showing up at his estate." Could this be true? Perhaps.

The Pritzker family is one of the top ten richest families in the United States and made their wealth in the Hyatt hotel chain. J.B. Pritzker is the current Governor of Illinois and owns a private venture capital firm, The Pritzker Group. It was revealed in May of 2020 that this family investment firm owns stake in two companies that were creating COVID19 tests. Pritzker was boasting how Illinois was testing the most residents per capita among the most populated states. Pritzker kept the state of Illinois under a mandatory mask order for over eleven months and locked down the state for even longer. Meanwhile, he shipped his family off to their other home in Geneva, Wisconsin and estate in Florida. Most of the Pritzker family does not live in Illinois. J.B. Pritzker also financed the Clinton campaigns.

James Pritzker a retired lieutenant colonel for the United States Army is now a transgender who goes by the name "Jennifer". Real sister, Penny Pritzker, is a member of the Trilateral Commission and has connections to the Council on Foreign Relations. Penny is worth over two billion dollars herself and served as the Secretary of Commerce under Barack Obama. Anthony Pritzker, J.B.'s brother, works for the Rand Corporation. On the same day J.B. Pritzker signed the anti-harassment legislation, it came out of the unsealed court records that his cousin, Tom Pritzker, had ties to Jeffrey Epstein. Tom Pritzker was good friends with current Mayor Lori Lightfoot. Lori Lightfoot's wife, Amy, has philanthropic ties to Bill and Melinda Gates. See how these people all connect?

Ronald Lauder is the President of the Zionist World Jewish Congress. This congress was founded in Geneva, Switzerland as an international federation of Jewish communities. They also have special consultative status with the United Nations. The Chairman of the Board is David Rothschild. The Lauder family is connected to the Austrian House of Esterhazy and Ronald Lauder is Austrian. He is worth over four billion dollars. There are many Lauder family members who are prominent around the world in business and finance and members of the Bilderberg Group.

Michael Bloomberg is a top player in the Zionist game and worth over 50 billion dollars. It is safe to bet that he may run the Zionist Mafia, at least in the United States. Jack Dorsey founder and CEO of Twitter once said that his idol is Michael Bloomberg. Bloomberg ran for president against Donald Trump in 2020 and used to frequent the Vatican to have meetings with the Bavarian Pope Benedict XVI.

If you want to know who the players are look no further than professional sports owners. Robert Kraft (New England Patriots), Mark Cuban (Dallas Mavericks), Dan Gilbert (Cleveland Cavaliers), George Kaiser (OKC Thunder), Jerry Reinsdorf (Chicago Bulls and White Sox), and Joshua Harris (Philadelphia 76ers). Joshua Harris also co-owns Apollo Global Management which financed Jared Kushner with over 180 million dollars for Kushner Companies. Jared Kushner's father, Charles, was convicted of illegal tax evasion and witness tampering through attempted blackmail.

Charles Kushner hired a prostitute to seduce his brother-in-law. As of 2020, President Donald Trump pardoned Charles.

You can also look into owners of top casinos in America and all over the world. Entertainment is ruled by the Jewish Mafia. Other Zionist run companies are in oil, drilling, finance, banking, chemicals, big pharma, energy and shipping.

The Sackler family owns Purdue Pharma and are responsible for getting the entire world addicted to OxyContin. They have been producing and pushing this drug in the medial industry for decades and have created one of the worst epidemics in the history of big pharma. The Zionist agenda falls right in line with the New World Order, keep everyone sick or make them believe they are sick.

Walmart, the monopoly of all monopolies, is run by Jewish Zionists. Samuel Walton has a net worth of over 47 billion dollars and is the primary owner of Walmart. If you notice the Walmart logo it has the six-pointed star just like the Zionist logo. Many of the Walton family are Jesuit educated and connected to the Jewish Guggenheim family.

Walmart logo and Zionist six-pointed star

The Durst family are known to their development of numerous building in New York City such as the One World Trade Center. This family is worth over four billion dollars and one of the family members is Robert Durst, remember him? He was suspected of killing at least three people including his wife, Kathleen and later on, two more to cover up the murder of his wife. HBO released a miniseries about Robert Durst called The Jinx where it tells the story from his point of view. In the series he is friends with Susan Berman whose father was a mobster who replaced Bugsy Seigel and the Genovese crime family at Las Vegas' Flamingo hotel. Robert Durst was found not guilty even though he admitted to beheading and dismembering his victims in the miniseries. These people are extremely corrupt and well connected.

The Christian Zionists believe that the modern state of Israel is a result of biblical prophecy. It centers around the idea that 4,000 years ago God promised the land to the Jews, who will rule until Jesus' return to Jerusalem and the time of the rapture. Christian Zionists believe all Christians will be saved while everyone who doesn't convert to Christianity will be sent to hell. Christian Zionists believe that God will only support those who support Israel. They believe they are not only curbing anti-Semitism but contributing to the salvation of the world and the completion of God's redemptive plans. But to keep it real, it provides a map for the future and major world control.

This is a very complex and deep issue, where parts of the religion are ignored for political gain and parts of politics are ignored to fulfil the theology. Which brings me to the Israeli/Palestinian conflict. In a nutshell, this is the world's longest running and most controversial conflict. At its heart, it is between two self-determined movements, the Jewish/Christian Zionists and the Palestinian nationalist project, who both lay claim to the same territory, which is described as the Holy Land. Included in this territory is the West bank.

Israel gets much media attention, sympathy and support from the Trump administration (2016-2020). It is Palestinian Christians and Jews who challenge this dominant narrative. But because of the powers that be, the Palestinians don't have a real voice or any media reach. And let's not forget it was Nixon who assured the Israeli prime minister that he was extremely sympathetic to Israel, which really sealed the deal for his presidency. Here are a few popular Christian Zionists that you may recognize. Billy Graham, Kirk Cameron, Joel Osteen, Tammy Faye, John Hagee. The Trump administration makes policy and manages the federal government through the combined efforts of two distinct groups: a group of radicalized Christian Zionists who are super rich and the alienated working-class families in the United States.

In 2014, the Washington Post reported that Sheldon Adelson's strategy for the 2016 presidential race was to support a mainstream candidate capable of winning the presidency. Adelson had one on one meetings with John Kasich, Jeb Bush, Chris Christie, Scott Walker and Donald Trump. Trump won his support and on May 13, Adelson pledged 100 million dollars to the Trump campaign. It was reported in August of 2020 that Trump made a call to Adelson complaining he had not done enough for him. After that call, Adelson pledged a $200 million dollar donation.

To understand Christian Zionism, you must realize that we are talking about the evangelicals. How many times have you heard Trump talk about the evangelicals? Betsy Devos, a member of the 88th richest billionaire family in America, is considered an "elder" of her Christian evangelical megachurch in Michigan. Her brother, Erik Prince, was the CEO of Blackwater, who scored over two billion dollars in CIA classified contracts with the Clinton administration through Obama.

The New York Times reported that Erik Prince arranged a meeting in May 2018 with Don Jr., George Nader and Joel Zamel which had to do with Saudi Arabia and Israeli interests. Robert Mercer, an American billionaire who was one of the first researchers and developers of artificial intelligence was the primary benefactor of the Make America Number One super pac. This pac employed Kellianne Conway and Steve Bannon. Mercer donated 15.5 million to the 2016 campaign.

Trump claims to be Presbyterian which is evangelical. And whether you noticed or not, he caters to his super rich, white evangelical base through the US embassy move to Jerusalem, support for Israeli annexation of the Golan Heights and the West Bank, and through his choice for VP, evangelical Mike Pence. Christian Zionism is a very successful but unlikely interfaith movement, but it is pushing forth a shift in the nature of government to feel revolutionary when it in fact, is not. This shift in ideologies has been obscured to ordinary Americans because all of the media sources are essentially edited by the same super-rich people who are leading this progress.

2020 showed us that a faction of the super-rich has poured billions of dollars, seen and unseen to take apart the federal government, take over our local government and render it as a tool to collect more money from taxpayers for the use of their corporations and agendas. This favored approach creates the hyped crises that permits the transfer of huge sums of money to either prop up or crash the stock market. 9/11 and the coronavirus pandemic are the best representatives of this approach.

And over time, these elites bought and cultivated politicians, intellectuals and talking heads and used them to convince Americans that government is always harmful, and decriminalization brings freedom! They have marketed entrepreneurialism and sells the idea that anyone who tries can be equally wealthy. Very few do this with the help of inheritance. This myth, this American dream is just a lie, for the ordinary citizen. And I believe the super-rich will be cashing in even more with the coronavirus vaccine, contact tracing, immunity passports and more. I don't think there is any way to stop this train.

This is what I mean when I say President Trump could be controlled. I believe he is in over his head now. These elites do not care about policy; all they care about is making a profit at the expense of the world. It is important to note that much of this policy is not about Donald Trump himself. Although his political persona is tough and narcissistic at times, his demands as president suggest that he has a bravery that has never been seen before. There is no denying that. The point is not to make Trump look good, but rather to avoid any significant policy debate. Making Trump look foolish is a major part of the Christian Zionist strategy. We do know that the media itself has become such a part of the corporate world that it is not capable of offering any critical analysis of what Trump is trying to do.

What we are witnessing today is a tiny handful of the super-rich trying to establish a shadow government that makes all actions: executive, judicial and congressional, a major part of their agenda to promote their own wealth. They are not necessarily the friends of Donald Trump and would throw him under the bus or kill him, if it suited their purposes. Many players among the Christian Fascists are not covered by the media at all, citizens have a difficult time figuring out what is going on. Trump is described as the orange bad man in the media and made the target of attack. He is vilified, but the major players among the super-rich and the Christian fascists remain virtually unknown to the public and their impact on Trump's policy is completely ignored.

The growing power of the Christian fascists, whose megachurches are sprinkled over much of rural and suburban America, can only be understood in the context of the ideological, economic and social collapse that is taking place across the country. There is no longer any vision for what the United States is and what its purpose should be. And now post-coronavirus there is no longer any civil society, no town halls in which citizens meet together for a common purpose at the local level. There are no activities that affirm the commitment of citizens to each other or to society. All the media is focused on death, fear, consumption, the cult of the self and COVID19 "cures".

The coronavirus pandemic has led to the destruction of local communities has been combined with the destruction of local business, local industry and local farming by corporations, to such a degree that what were once strong communities offering mutual support are now cultural and social deserts. This deep social and economic destruction offers Christian right-wing groups an opportunity to exploit people, especially poorly educated, impoverished whites in rural and suburban areas. The Christian Zionists, especially evangelicals, established churches in these regions that provide the basic needs for education, economic opportunity, and a sense of meaning in the lives of these alienated citizens. These megachurches are becoming the effective government for large parts of the country, offering services that no one else will.

Many poorer whites find that they have no option but to join up with these churches to survive economically and spiritually. The churches are run for profit like a McDonald's, and they control carefully what the members are told through teachings at churches and the television that they watch. If you pay attention, you will notice that the attendees are told to support Republicans, and to give full support to Donald Trump.

The teachings given out in these churches are a modified form of Christianity. They have removed from their teaching all the parts from Christianity about helping the poor and about creating an egalitarian society. In place of charity and grace, the Christian Zionists place an emphasis on preparing for a world war and destruction before the return of Jesus to save them.

Christian Zionists believe that the end of the world is coming soon. That things will be "biblical". Where have we heard that before? They have promoted the idea of the rapture through movies and tv shows and only the true Christians will be saved by Jesus. These evangelical Christians (best represented in the Trump administration by Mike Pompeo and Mike Pence, who make security policy decisions and then inform Trump of what they have done) believe that the Jews must return to Jerusalem, establish a powerful Israel there, and build a third temple there in Jerusalem and await the end of days. For them, the destruction of humanity is not only guaranteed, it is something to be welcomed.

They believe that when Jesus returns to save them, the Jews who were necessary to build the temple to fulfill scripture will not be saved. Rather, although they served their purpose, Jews, and Israel specifically, will be tossed into Hell because they do not accept Jesus.

The most powerful Christian Zionist faction supported by these churches is the group known as Christians United for Israel. Christians United for Israel claims a membership of seven million, larger than any Jewish organization. This group also claims that "Christians have a biblical obligation to defend Israel." Christians United for Israel is run by John Hagee, the most powerful leader among the Christian Zionists and a visible figure in right-wing politics.

John Hagee runs a mega-church in Texas, and he uses this Christian Zionist network to take in funding and push a clearly defined ideology among his followers. He pushes for war on every front, working closely with the far right in Israel. His Global Evangelism Television (GETV) is the main source for news for most of these Christians. As a news source that glorifies war, that declares all enemies of Israel the enemies of God and that suggests that a world war focused on Israel is necessary to bring Jesus back for the rapture, it is a deeply disturbing source of propaganda. It should be noted that Hagee works closely with Zionist billionaire Sheldon Adelson.

As far as policy, their closest ally is Mike Pompeo, the Secretary of State. Pompeo has been promoted in politics because of his support from these

Christians and he has been absolutely loyal to them. In my opinion, Trump is becoming increasingly a prisoner of their network. It is also my belief this group wishes for Trumps resignation so Pence will take over. It is also my belief they had control over Attorney General William Barr and members of the Supreme court. Bill Barr left office in December of 2020 after contradicting his claims that the election was stolen from Trump.

The greatest challenge in the United States today is not responding to the specific actions of Donald Trump or Mike Pompeo. The current pattern promoted by the corporate media is the constant encouragement of staying mad at Trump, calling him a racist and a narcissist. And in return Trump yells "fake news" even though he knows his people are behind it. I believe that we are facing not only a religious war but are in desperate need of an alternative ideology. We need a formation of institutions with a shared sense of values. We need smaller government, more community. We need to breakdown and eliminate these religious organizations and realize the real damage they are doing. And if we don't the Christian Zionist movement will only grow stronger.

When we think about the mark of the beast and what it is, you have to understand that this could be a big trick by the Zionists. Have you ever stopped to wonder, maybe this is a test? For they provide the mark and those who take it deserve to die? Based on their reformed modern beliefs and their stretching of religious dogmas this scenario would not shock me.

I know most YouTube channels that discuss Trump are Pro-Trump or pushing the Q narrative. But they just don't go deep enough. You can analyze his press conferences all day and night. You can analyze the insanity of Joe Biden and Kamala Harris. But people fail to search for who they are backed by. When you really look deep into Trump and you see how deeply rooted his backers are, it is easy to see how he was able to do many positive things prior to coronavirus, because the evangelicals supported these ideas. Is Christian Zionism bad? That is up to you to decide. Whenever people hear me say that, they immediately call me a conspiracy theorist or crazy.

Some people do believe this is the end times prophecy. And accepting these new norms is accepting the mark of the beast. And before I go, let me ask you one question. Do you think the Christian Zionists who so strongly believe in the rapture, the end time Revelations prophecy, will be accepting this mark themselves?

JESUITS

"I'm not saying everyone who is Catholic is bad, but there is a criminal faction within the Catholic church, who call themselves the Jesuits, which is the intelligence arm of the Vatican."

Have you ever wondered why there is an overwhelming number of liberal arts colleges? Have you ever wondered why Greek life exists? Greek Fraternities and Sororities have a been a symbol of college life for centuries. Did you know, over 80% of the executives of fortune 500 companies are fraternity men? More than 3/4s of the United States senators are fraternity men. And 40 out of the 47 United States Supreme Court Justices since 1910 are fraternity men. Is this a coincidence? If an employer sees Greek fraternity on your resume does it give you an advantage? How and why did Greek life become so prominent on college campuses? The answer to these questions directs us straight to the Black Nobility House of Farnese.

The **House of Farnese** established the society of Jesus otherwise known as the Jesuits as a military order through the papal bull; under Pope Paul the 3rd whose name was Alessandro Farnese. The leader of the Jesuits is called the Superior General or the "black pope." The first black pope was Ignatius of Loyola in 1539. Before Loyola was the black pope, he was a member of the Alumbrados, the Spanish illuminati; the precursor to Adam Weishaupt's Bavarian Illuminati which he started in 1776. Loyola was obsessed with fame and had a reputation of being a narcissist.

Under the House of Farnese, Loyola's mission was to infiltrate and reform the Protestant and Catholic churches. Loyola established the "Methods of prayer" otherwise known as the "spiritual exercises" which are still used today. The Spiritual exercises stemmed from mystical and Hermetic practices which enable demonic control.

Hermetic magic is a type of black magic that originated from ancient Egyptians and was portrayed in the book of the dead. Rene d Anjou, a descendant of the Merovingian bloodline persuaded Cosimo Medici of the Black Nobility House of Medici family, to establish a library at San Marco where Plato, Pythagorean works and books on Hermetic magic were translated. It was from Cosimo Medici's library that sparked up the Greek and Egyptian teachings by the Jesuits that influenced the Italian Renaissance.

The Jesuits have been responsible for major deception and murder throughout history. In the book, "The suppressed truth about the assassination of Abraham Lincoln", the author claims that the powerful Giacomo Antonelli, a Cardinal and Secretary of the Papal States under Pope Pius 9th, supervised the plot to kill Abraham Lincoln with help of the Jesuits. Notice the hidden hand. And we all know about the JFK conspiracy involving the mafia and Black Nobility connections and that would be an entire video in itself.

Charles Chiniquy, a Catholic priest, wrote in his memoir that the Jesuits killed Lincoln. He believed there was a conspiracy between the Vatican and the Jesuits to take control of the United States by importing certain powerful Catholics from Black Nobility families. He eventually denounced the Catholic church and left, saying it was anti-Christian and pagan at its core.

In 1599, the Ratio Studiorum was written by academics at the Jesuit Roman College established by Loyola. This "Jesuit plan of education" is a document that standardized the Jesuit education and was the precursor to the Liberal Studies that have been instituted in all colleges and Universities. 100 years after the Jesuits were established, they were running almost 700 schools. The Jesuit missionaries traveled all over the world establishing liberal arts education. The Jesuit China missions brought Western Science and astronomy and it was the Jesuits who popularized "Confucius" and had a huge influence on the Chinese enlightenment. The Ratio Studiorum was revised in 1832 but still centered around the liberal studies of science, social science, arts and humanities.

In 1820, Luigi Fortis was elected the "black pope". During his short term in office, he spent it institutionalizing the Jesuit plan of education into colleges in Europe, Canada and the United States. And since 1825, all but two US Presidents and US Vice presidents have been Fraternity men. Union college, a private, male only school in New York established Kappa Alpha, the first fraternity. Since 1795, 19 US presidents have attended this school. Two years after the birth of Kappa Alpha, Sigma Phi and Delta Phi were established. This triad referred to themselves as "Fraternities" which derives from the Latin word "Frater" meaning "brother." The Jesuit established fraternities started spreading to other campuses, national chapters were created and that is how Greek life in the United States began.

In 1851, the first two official women's secret societies were founded at Wesleyan college in Macon, Georgia. They were called the Adelphean society and the Philomathean society. It wasn't until 1900 these secret societies became the sororities Alpha Delta Pi and Phi Mu. Sorority comes from the Latin word Soror meaning "sister."

There are many collegiate elite secret societies in the United States, and they make a significant effort to keep the affairs and initiations secret. The first collegiate secret society was the Fat Hat Club created in 1750 at the College of William and Mary in Williamsburg, Virginia. President Thomas Jefferson was a member. Thomas Jefferson also wrote favorably about Adam Weishaupt, the founder of the Bavarian Illuminati and a Jesuit professor. Although Weishaupt was the front man for the Luciferian organization, he was actually backed and funded by the Black Nobility Farnese family.

It was the House of Farnese who elevated the Rothschilds into power and moved the Farnese family seat of power to Washington DC. This family Is one of the most powerful families on Earth today. The Farnese family built their Pentagon fortress known as Villa Caprarola in Lazio, Italy. In their map room, which was designed in the 1500's, includes a painting of the world showing the continent Antarctica. Did you know that Antarctica was not officially discovered until the 1770's. This was around the same time the Farnese family recruited Adam Weishaupt to create the illuminati and moved the Farnese seat of power to Washington DC, where they built their second pentagon. How did the Farnese family know about Antarctica? Interesting to note that the Washington capital is placed between Virginia and Maryland. Did you know that Larry Farnese, a member of this family, is a state senator for Pennsylvania?

In the book, Rulers of Evil, Tupper Saussy explains how Washington DC was built on land that was owned by the Jesuit educated, Daniel Carroll of the very rich and powerful Carroll family. Daniel's brother, John Carroll, was a Jesuit priest and the founder of Jesuit college Georgetown University. John Carroll was the priest of Pierre Charles L'Enfant, the man who was hired to design Washington DC with occult symbology.

Jesuit alumni dominate leadership positions in US military and intelligence as well as politics and law. The Farnese family ruled Parma and Castro of Italy and today the Princes of Bourbon-Parma covertly have authority in the US Pentagon and US military through their Jesuit intelligence. And it is the Italian **Black Nobility** families who control Hollywood and the media.

Did you know that Hitler was extremely anti-Jesuit and considered them to be the most dangerous enemy? Over 200 Jesuits were murdered by Nazi's in Europe.

It is interesting to note that most people believe the Jesuits are one in the same with the Catholic church, but they are not. They are actually at odds with each other. There is an on-going tense relationship between them over disagreements about abortion, birth control and gay marriage among other things. The Jesuits are in favor of far-left politics, particularly Marxism. And the conspiracy that the Jesuits have infiltrated the Catholic church is more than obvious. And now the current pope Francis is the first Jesuit pope. He served under the black pope before he became head of the Vatican.

I understand it might be difficult for some people to believe that the Jesuits could be a sinister group. But we must understand what the Jesuits believe and who put them in power. The Spiritual exercises taught by Loyola were based on mystical alchemical practices.

In Jesuit collegiate secret societies, the words "Circuli Crux Non Orbis Prosunt" are displayed for all to see and memorize. This is an alchemical expression which translates to "the diameter of the sphere, the tau of the circle, and the cross of the orbit do not benefit the blind." This means that these Jesuit esoteric disciplines are not accessible to the uninitiated. The diameter of the sphere is the symbol of the saltpeter (nitric acid); the tau of the circle is the symbol for Vitriol and the cross of the globe is the symbol for antimony; the atomic number 51; a semi metal.

This Egyptian symbology is also found on the Alchemical door aka the alchemy gate or the magic portal, that still stands in Rome at the old residence of Massimiliano Palombara. This door dates back to the 1600's. Palombara was a kabbalist and mystic who was sought out by Catholic Cardinal Decio Azzolini who was the leader of the Squadrone Volante. This group of liberal cardinals were looking for enlightenment. There are many legends of people going through the magic portal door, disappearing forever but leaving behind flakes of gold.

Hermes invented the process of making a glass tube airtight which is the process of magic alchemy using a secret seal. Mysticism is the religious practice of alternate state of consciousness through contemplative prayer. Hermeticism is an esoteric tradition based on the teaching of Hermes. Hermes is the ancient Greek deity known as the psychopomp, who helps guide deceased souls into the afterlife. And it was these esoteric teachings by Hermes that led to the birth of the Renaissance, the development of science, alchemy and magic. The 17th century also saw the rise of esoteric societies such as the Rosicrucian's and Freemasons. The famous motto of the Rosicrucian's is the acronym for Vitriol meaning "Visit the interior of the earth, working with righteousness you will find the hidden stone". This expression indicates the need to descend into the dark ravines of the soul to initiate one self's spirit into immortality and bring light to wisdom.

Freemasons make use of the acronym VITRIOL as it is imprinted on the Masonic dark wall where the person must stay before being affiliated. The seal of VITRIOL is the most complete representation of the alchemical process also known as "the great work" or the "Magnus Opus". There are four stages to the Great work. 1) Nigredo, associated with the earth element, symbolized by the crow, winter, Saturn and order out of chaos. 2) Albedo is associated with the element of water, symbolized by the swan, Moon, the feminine and Spring. 3) Citinitas associated with the element air, symbolized by the eagle, the sun, the masculine and Summer. And 4)

Rubedo, associated with the element fire, symbolized by the phoenix, the androgynous fusion between male and female, the alchemical wedding. It has been said that the rainbow "peacock tail" is a symbol of the wide range of colors that can be seen after this alchemical process. Where have we seen this before (NBC). And after the initiate goes through the seven phases of the vitriol is when they become the "ONE" symbolized by the downward triangle.

The Monita Secreta otherwise known as the secret instructions of the society is a Machiavellian instruction manual on the art of dissimilation and manipulation in the pursuit of money and power. Some say it was written by Claudio Aquaviva, the fifth pope, while some scholars claim it was written by ex-Jesuit Jerome Zahorwski. The manual itself is chilling to read. One line that stuck out me to read, "those who do not love us, shall fear us." Did the Jesuits write this? Or was this written by rogue Jesuit? Does it matter who wrote it? The fact is someone wrote it. It makes me remember Loyola's obsession with fame, what he accomplished in life and the power he had over the entire world, including his connections with the Black Nobility.

The Roman House of Farnese was at one time, the most powerful Roman family in the history. The Farnese's ruled when the Jesuits were established and built a pentagonal mansion in Caprarola, Italy which was the architectural basis for the United States Pentagon. The Jesuit's headquarters, the Gesu Church, which is in Rome, has the name Farnese engraved on the top of their church. The House of Farnese dissolved in 1766 but assimilated into the House of Bourbon through the marriage of Elizabeth Farnese and the House of Bourbon King Philip the fifth of Spain. This transfer of power made the House of Bourbon the new powerhouse. Carl Mayor von Rothschild, was born under the House of Bourbon, started the Rothschild banking of Naples. He lent the Vatican over five million starting in 1832. Since then, the Rothschilds have been the fiscal agents of the Vatican. The Rothschild-Vatican cabal unsuccessfully took over American banks during the Revolutionary war and the 1812 war. This is all due to the protection of the constitution. But the Rothschild-Vatican cabal succeeded with the establishment of the Federal Reserve Act in 1913 under President Woodrow Wilson.

The Society of Jesus otherwise known as the Jesuits were established by Ignatius of Loyola under the Vatican, through the papal bull military regiment in 1540. What most people don't know about the is that the Jesuits were expelled over and over again from almost every Catholic European country in the 1700's. Charles the third expelled the Jesuits from all Spanish-controlled territories in 1767 because he felt they had acquired too much power, wealth and influence. The HURON native American tribe of Canada accused the Jesuits of putting spells on them and blamed them for the disease outbreaks in their communities. However, no matter how many times the Jesuits were expelled they always found a way back in, to renew their work after the chaos they created, subsided. And it is this fact, that is the proof, that there is something morally wrong with the Jesuits.

In 1916, Senator Robert Owen stated, "the United States is the prime target to which the Vatican directs the subversive and destructive activities of the Jesuits." Jesuit training lasts anywhere from 8-14 years and by the time the priests are thrown back out into the world they are highly brainwashed
Jesuit Rule 13 reads: That we may be altogether of the same mind and conformity." In other words, do not think for yourself and follow blindly. Historian R Healey stated, "The Jesuits are so extreme in their submission they become like machines-their determination to achieve their goals drew on powers unavailable to other men, through black magic. If Jesuits speak about the works of the Jesuits, they will find themselves assassinated."

After researching the Jesuits, I realized that they are actually victims of brainwashing and mind control. The Jesuits are the world's Manchurian candidates, which in my mind makes them one of the most misunderstood groups in the world. They are evil no doubt, but they are also victims of the globalist control. According to the book *Vatican Assassins* by Eric John Phelps, the man responsible for ordering assassinations, terror attacks and wars in the underworld is none other than the Black Pope, the unofficial name for the Superior General of the Jesuits. It has been written that they call him the "Black Pope" as a tribute to their use of Black magic. Black magic comes from the Great White Brotherhood or the ascended masters. The black pope takes its orders from the Vatican and I find it interesting that pope Francis is the first Jesuit Pope.

There is an overwhelming amount of Jesuit educated people running the biggest companies' banks and political positions in our country. The World Bank Group, Goldman Sachs, Morgan Stanley, Bank of England and the European Central Bank are all run by Jesuit educated people. Jesuits have run the IRS and NASA. Jesuit educated CIA directors include Robert Gates, George Tenet, Leon Panetta, Michael Morell, David Petraeus and John Brennan. Former CIA Director James Clapper was a professor at Jesuit Georgetown University. Georgetown is the oldest Jesuit college in America and holds the Jesuit traditions while being extremely selective in who they choose to enroll. They take pride in the fact that many of their graduates go on to be leaders on the world stage.

Seven out of the nine Supreme Court Justices that sit on the Supreme Court were all Jesuit educated and members of the Jesuit Fraternity, Phi Beta Kappa. Vanderbilt professor Donald Davidson claimed that Phi Beta Kappa was a Marxist fraternity and heavily influenced by communism ideals.

Joe Biden has two Jesuit honorary degrees. Hunter Biden attended Georgetown and served as a Jesuit volunteer after he graduated. Donald Trump, Donald Trump Jr., Ivanka Trump, Eric Trump, Tiffany Trump, Bill Clinton, the Podesta Brothers, Steve Bannon, Steven Miller, Paul Manafort, King Abduallah II, King Felipe VI of Spain, Crown Prince Pavlos of Greece, Prince of Luxembourg, Pierre and Justin Trudeau, John Kerry, John Boehner, Robert Redfield (head of the Center for Disease Control), Anthony Fauci, Jay Powell (Chairman of the Federal Reserve), Gavin Newsome, the Cuomo brothers, Mike Madigan (Chicago Mafia), and James Walton of the Walmart dynasty. Most all of them graduated from Georgetown University.

If we go back in history: Joseph Goebbel, the head of Nazi propaganda, Joseph Stalin was trained by Jesuit Monks, Fidel Castro, Brzezinski the psychopath who warned us about the technocrat society, Lyndon Johnson, Prescott Bush, Mark Dybul the Global Aids Coordinator who worked closely with Anthony Fauci, and I would also like to point out that there were 36 people in the Bush administration that were Jesuit educated who handled the aftermath of 9/11.

History tells us that Jesuit agents were infiltrating countries all the way back to the 1700's so you would have to assume there are Jesuit agents in our country today. After I released my research on the Jesuits and recorded several podcasts, I started receiving many messages from men who were Jesuits institutions. One message read, "I was in a Jesuit school for a decade. You are right on the money about them."

VATICAN

"The devil resides in the Vatican."

The Vatican is a city state whose official name is "Stato della Citta del Vaticano". It is considered the spiritual headquarters of the Roman and Catholic churches under the sovereign rule of the Pope. The ecclesiastical entity of the Vatican is known as the Holy See. The Holy See (See of Rome) is the jurisdiction of the Bishop of Rome (pope) which governs international law.

The Vatican is the smallest country in the world encircled by a two-mile border with Italy. Vatican City is an independent city-state making it one-eighth the size of New York's Central Park. The Vatican became independent from Italy with the Lateran Treaty of 1929 and is owned by the Black Nobility, specifically, the House of Bourbon-Two Sicilies.

The word Vatican is derived from *Vatica/Vaticum* from the name of an Etruscan settlement or general area the Romans called *Ager Vaticanus* (Vatican territory). *Ager Vaticanus* etymology suggests the name came from the childbirth deity *Vaticanus* or *Vagitanus*, the god of the *Vagiti* wailings.

Inside Vatican City sits the Vatican Obelisk, which was originally taken by Caligula, the third Roman Emperor, from the city of Heliopolis in Egypt. Obelisks were called 'tekhenu' by ancient Egyptians and are considered monolithic. The Obelisk was modeled after the sun god Ra and during the religious reformation of Akhenaten. The sun god Ra was the Egyptian's greatest deity. Ra was believed to rule all parts of the world: the sky, the Earth and the underworld. He was the god of the sun, order, kings and the sky. All forms of life were believed to have been created by Ra and the Egyptians called themselves the "cattle of Ra".

The Vatican is an absolute monarchy and the Pope exercises legislative, executive and judicial power over Vatican City. Vatican City is one of the few independent states that has not become a member of the United

Nations but has a permanent observer status over the United Nations General Assembly. The United Nations was established after WWII with the aim of preventing future wars and their objectives have been to maintain international peace, promote sustainable development and uphold international law. The Vatican also has permanent observer status over the European Union, OSCE, Organization of American States (OAS), the World Health Organization (WHO) and the World Trade Organization (WTO).

The United States is a federal corporation under U.S. Code 3002, section 15. The 14th amendment states that anyone born in the jurisdiction of the United States are subject to the United States which is defined as a corporation. George Washington, Alexander Hamilton, John Hancock and Benjamin Franklin were all Freemasons working under the Grand Lodge of England for the House of Guelph (now house of Windsor). The Virginia Company (United States) was transformed into the United States of America in 1776 during the Revolutionary war.

Novus Ordo Seclorum is Latin and translates to New Order of the Ages and is on the United States Great Seal and United States one-dollar federal reserve note. Novus Ordo Seclorum was added to the dollar in 1935 which is six years after the Vatican City was established as a sovereign nation. The Vatican is employed by many members of the Black Nobility families and the Rothschilds have been the fiscal agents of the Vatican since the 1800's. It is interesting to point out that much of the United States architecture was modeled after Rome. Capitol Hill in Washington D.C. is architecturally based on Saint Peter's Basilica and named after Capitoline Hill in Rome. The House of Torlonia serve as the Vatican's treasurers and the United States Treasury building is modeled after the House of Torlonia Villa in Rome. The House of Farnese Villa Caprarola is a Pentagonal fortress which established the Jesuits and was the architectural basis for the United States Pentagon. The Jesuits of Georgetown dominate leadership positions at the United States Pentagon. Coincidence?

The Catholic church has a systemic problem of sexual abuse of children and nuns. A 2019 documentary, Sex Slaves in the Catholic Church, was banned from broadcast in Europe. It is a story about a group of French nuns who claim they were used as sex slaves by priests and were forced to abort every pregnancy. When the nuns addressed this issue to Pope Francis and the Vatican in 2015, they were denied and silenced. The priests of 23 countries are still abusing to this day.

It also should be noted that Pope Francis (Jorge Mario Bergoglio) is the first Jesuit Pope in history. Like many Jesuits that came before him, he amended God's words and made theological changes based on his own personal beliefs. For example, he suggested that legally recognizing same sex marriage is crucial and showed support for LGBT ideas. He has protected pedophile priests. He has argued that divorced people who civilly remarry should be able to receive penance and the Eucharist. Pope Francis cooperated with the Chinese Communist Party to normalize "Chinese Catholics" but was criticized by Cardinal Joseph Zen and Mike Pompeo. Pope Francis was also against Donald Trump's wall and said, "building walls is not of the gospel". Pope Francis also tried to encourage Donald Trump to remain in the Paris Agreement. Pope Francis was also the first Pope to create an Instagram account and obtained over one million followers in under twelve hours.

Pope Francis' Coat of Arms is depicted by the crest, the Bishop's mitre, the IHS Christogram (Holy Name of Jesus), keys of Peter, the Jesuit emblem and the shield, red cross, eight-pointed star and the flower that represents Saint Joseph (branch of spikenard).

Pope Francis Coat of Arms

Pope Francis has been photographed wearing some questionable symbolism. His robe has the universal "boy love" pedophile symbol.

Pope Francis' staff resembles the symbolism on the Baphomet statue. Baphomet is the winged, goat headed humanoid which represents the occult for the Satanic temple. The statue stands 8.5 feet tall, features a prominent pentagram and is the mere suggestion of separation of church and state. The bronze Baphomet statue was unveiled in Detroit in 2015.

Pope Francis: Jesuit and Freemason

The Vatican has an observatory manned by Jesuit astronomers and there has been conspiracy over the name of their telescope. The Large Binocular Telescope was originally called LUCIFER which stood for Large Binocular Telescope Near-infrared Spectroscopic Utility with Camera and Integral Field Unit for Extragalactic Research. In 2012, they changed the name to LUCI. What's even more odd besides the Vatican's interest in outer space are the articles written about UFO sightings over Italy and the Vatican since the 1970's.

In December of 1978, dozens of people witnessed a doughnut-shaped aircraft spewing a green light above Rome and coincidentally enough there was an influx of missing people in that area. There were other documented sightings from 1978 to 2005 and there were suggestions that these had to do with a 900-year-old prophecy by Saint Malachy of the return of Apollo, whom the elite believe will rule the final holy empire.

From a 2010 article titled, *Pope's Exorcist Says the Devil is in the Vatican*, Reverend Gabriel Amorth said, "The devil is not everywhere, but when he is present it is painful. I have treated over 70,000 cases of demonic possession. The devil is pure spirit, invincible. He is shown with the painful blasphemies coming from the person which he possesses. He can stay hidden. He can speak different languages. He can transform himself. None of this scares me, I know that God is using me for this work. The devil took a strike in the Vatican in 1981 by attacking John Paul II and the attack on Christmas Eve when the crazy woman pushed down Benedict XVI. The devil resides in the Vatican."

The founder of the CIA, William Donovan, was knighted by two Vatican orders. Rupert Murdoch, founder of NewsCorp and runs Fox News is a Vatican Knight of Saint Gregory. Roy Disney was a Knight of Saint Gregory. Frank Shakespeare, ex-president of CBS was a Vatican knight. John Raskob who built the Empire State Building was a Knight of Saint Gregory.

The Propaganda Due (P2) was a Masonic Lodge under the Grand Orient of Italy. The P2 was referred to as a "state within a state" or "shadow government". The Vatican was connected to this lodge. Licio Gelli, an Italian financier and Fascist was a Master of the P2. It was written that the CIA paid Gelli to instigate terrorist activities in Italy which involved the Vatican treasury.

If you are familiar with the "art" in the Vatican, you will see that it does not look so "holy". The statue of resurrection that sits behind the pope was created by sculptor Fazzini. He admits it is not designed to fit everyone's taste. Fazzini designed it to represent Jesus rising above a nuclear holocaust, desperation and sin. The statue is 66 feet tall and took six years to make. It was completed in 1977 during a time when "nuclear war" was more prevalent or worrisome.

Statue of Resurrection by Fazzini

The audience hall at the Vatican or otherwise known as the Hall of the Pontifical Audiences was designed by Italian architect Pier Luigi Nervi and was completed in 1971. It was built on land donated by the Knights of Columbus. Very interesting.

BILDERBERG GROUP

"Some even believe we are part of a secret cabal working against the best interests of the United States... If that's the charge, I stand guilty, and I am proud of it." - David Rockefeller

The Bilderberg meeting also known as the Bilderberg Group is an annual conference to foster the relationship between Europe and North America. The first meeting was held in 1954 by Prince Bernhard of the Netherlands at the Bilderberg hotel which is why they named themselves the Bilderberg's. Prince Bernhard belonged to the Nazi Party and was arguably the head of the Black Nobility before he died. John Foster Dulles was instrumental in getting the Bilderberg started and coincidentally he was the brother of Allen Dulles, the director of the CIA who helped orchestrate operation paperclip, which enabled a large number of Nazi scientists to avoid capital punishment and were put in positions in the United States government in various capacities.

It was during this meeting that the most powerful men in the world from the Dutch royal crown to the Rockefellers met for an entire weekend to discuss the future of the world. Since 1954, this elite group meets once a year in a different location to discuss the future of humanity and no media outlets or journalists are allowed to attend. It's been written that the Bilderberg's started with idealistic beginnings but morphed into a shadow world government with no transparency whatsoever. The members of the Bilderberg's are essentially all Nazis and keep the Nazi sentiments as the core of their agenda. Eugenics and population control are among some of their beliefs.

To give you an idea of the group I will read a quote from Daniel Estulin, who wrote the true story of the Bilderberg's. He stated, "It is a surreal world of double and triple agents, professional psychotic assassins, brainwashed black ops agents; a cesspool of duplicity and lies and doublespeak and innuendo and blackmail and bribery. These men's income are the dirtiest and most despicable government-run missions, the kind that can never be exposed." The Bilderberg's are the most secret of any powerful group and they select fringe people to report on subjects related to their agendas because they are completely clueless about the formal structure of the group and are ignorant to the group's greater goals and universal objectives.

Bill Clinton was a useful recruit. He attended his first Bilderberg meeting in 1991, in Germany. David Rockefeller explained to Clinton why NAFTA was a Bilderberg priority and that the group needed him to support it. That following year in 1992, Bill Clinton was elected president and pushed NAFTA to the forefront. Henry Kissinger was dubbed the "godfather" of the Bilderberg and has attended every meeting since the beginning. He is so committed to globalism he even wrote a book called "World Order."

The Bilderberg's have one main goal and that is to create a one world government or company that is financially regulated by one world bank using one global currency. They want to see nationalism eradicated. They want centralized control of the people. And they do this using mind control to get all of humanity to obey.

Members of the Bilderberg group are represented top figures from the Council on Foreign Relations, World Bank, Trilateral Commission, European Union, Central Bankers, Federal Reserve members and the Bank of England. Some of the more notable members are Henry Kissinger, Bill Clinton, Angela Merkel, Alan Greenspan, Ben Bernanke, George Soros, Donald Rumsfeld, Rupert Murdoch, Barack Obama, Hillary Clinton, Stacey Abrams, Jared Cohen (Founder of Alphabet), Jared Kushner, Matthew Pottinger, Mike Pompeo, Lindsay Graham, Wilbur Ross, Jeff Bezos, Bill Gates, Eric Schmidt, Peter Thiel, Charlie Rose, George Stephanopoulos and other heads of state, influential senators, selected media figures and writers, NATO members, congressmen and parliamentarians. Not to mention Kings and Queens of other countries.

Membership consists of around 80 annual attendees of the world's most powerful and others are invited occasionally due to their knowledge or involvement in relevant topics. The men and women who are most valued will be invited back. Some are first timers chosen for their possible future involvement.

It is a private club where members are not allowed to bring their husbands or wives or partners. Personal assistants, security, bodyguards, CIA or any other secret service cannot attend the conference. The guests are explicitly forbidden to give interviews or divulge any of the meeting criteria to the public. They are in an environment where everyone gets along, and they are allowed to say what they never dare say in public. NATO was essential for their success to ensure perpetual war and nuclear blackmail and would be used as necessary. They would then proceed to loot the planet, become even wealthier and crush any challenger who tried to oppose them. Along with military dominance, controlling all of the world's money is crucial for them. As Amschel Rothschild once said, "Give me control of a nation's money and I care not who makes the laws."

The Bilderberg group's master plan is for a One World Government with a single global marketplace, policed by one world army and a one world central bank. Daniel Estulin revealed in his book their wish list and now I'm going to read it.

1. To achieve one international identity, one set of universal values
2. Centralized control of world populations through mind control
3. No middle class, only rulers and serfs and no democracy
4. A zero-growth society
5. Manufactured crisis and wars
6. Absolute control of education
7. Centralized control of domestic and foreign policy
8. Expansion of NAFTA and the World Trade Organization
9. NATO will become a world military
10. Imposing a universal legal system
11. A global welfare state where obedient slaves will be rewarded, and non-conformists will be targeted for extermination.

The Bilderberg-Rockefeller alliance is to make their views "so appealing" that they become public policy so they can pressure world leaders into submitting. The media is their instrument to push their propaganda. Former CBS News president Richard Salant (1961 - 64 and 1966 - 79) explained the major media's role: "Our job is to give people not what they want, but what we decide they ought to have. What most Americans believe to be "public opinion" is actually carefully scripted propaganda designed to elicit desired behaviors from the public.

Perhaps one of the most important founders and members of the Bilderberg's, a foreign policy body of the Committee, was Józef Rettinger. Józef Rettinger was a well-trained Jesuit priest and a 33rd Degree Freemason knighted in the Order of the Garter. The other founders were David Rockefeller, Prince Bernard of the Netherlands and Dennis Healy. Healey was an extreme communist and once said, "World events do not occur by accident. They are made to happen, whether it is to do with national issues or commerce; and most of them are staged and managed by those who hold the purse strings."

The Bilderberg's understand that their success depends on finding ways to get us to surrender our liberties in the name of a common crisis. The target is and always will be individual liberty. They want an all-encompassing monopoly on property, industry, money and government and they will stop at nothing to attain it. In the world of big business: get a monopoly and let society work for you.

It is important to note the Bilderberg connection to the UFO/ET scenario. The American chapter of the Bilderberg group was started by Walter Bedell Smith who was head of the CIA at the time. It has been written that it is possible the Bilderberg's feel it is necessary to subdue the globe under one system before releasing extraterrestrial technologies.

In 2009, the Bilderberg's held their annual meeting in Greece and they were divided on two alternatives. The first would be a prolonged, tumultuous depression that dooms the world to decades of decline and poverty or a super-intense but shorter depression that paves the way for a new sustainable world order, with less sovereignty but more efficiency. They also discussed the future of the US dollar, continued deception about environmentalism, projecting United States unemployment, a final push for the Lisbon Treaty to adopt neoliberal rules, fewer work rights and open border trading. One of the Bilderberg's main concerns is the danger that their zeal to reshape the world by engineering chaos could cause the situation to spiral out of control and eventually lead to a scenario where

Bilderberg and the global elite are overwhelmed by events and end up losing their control over the planet.

During the 2009 meeting there was a combination of agreement and fear of the crises that lies ahead mainly because of America's extreme financial debt situation. They wanted to resolve this to produce a sustainable recovery. These topics included establishing a global treasury department and Global central bank, partnered with the International Monetary Fund or a global currency through destruction of the dollar. Their plan was to exploit the Swine Flu to create a World Health Organization for global health and to end national sovereignty.

Fast forward to 2019 and the meeting topics included: climate change and sustainability, China, Russia, the future of capitalism, Brexit, the weaponization of social media, the importance of space and cyber threats. Due to the Coronavirus pandemic the 2020 conference has been postponed but whether they will be successful in the future will be up to the citizens of the world.

CLUB OF ROME

"The threat is not climate crisis, for the real threat is the Club of Rome."

The Black Nobility established the Committee of 300 in the early eighteenth century and The Committee of 300 oversees many powerful organizations in the world and one of them is the Club of Rome which was established by Anglo-American bankers and the old Black Nobility families of Europe. The key to the successful control of the world is their ability to create and manage savage economic recessions and eventual depressions.

The Club of Rome was founded in 1968 by Aurelio Peccei and Alexander King who were both supporters of sustainable development. These two men believed that they were rebelling against the suicidal ignorance of the human condition. The Club of Rome was established as a non-profit organization which focuses on global warming and environmentalism. Its headquarters is in Switzerland. The Club of Rome's main purpose was to drive home the new world order by the year 2000. The Club of Rome works closely with Bilderberg Group, Trilateral commission, Council on Foreign Relations and Tavistock. These organizations are working together for the Black Nobility to promote Agenda 2030. Honorary members include Kings and Queens of the Black Nobility along with other world leaders.

The German Marshall Fund is an American think tank that funded and still funds the Club of Rome. These are two highly organized conspiratorial bodies operating under the North Atlantic Treaty Organization otherwise known as (NATO). The majority of Club of Rome executives have been drawn from NATO. All of NATO's policies are actually formulated by The Club of Rome which ultimately comes from the Committee of 300. Lord Peter Carrington, a British Conservative politician and the secretary general of NATO was able to split NATO into two factions, a political (left wing) power group and a military alliance. Lord Carrington was knighted by the Order of St. Michael and St. George.

As you learn about important figureheads that run these circles you will notice that most if not all of them have been knighted. The Club of Rome is still one of the most important foreign policy arms of the Committee of 300, next to the Bilderbergers.

The fake "environmentalist" movement was spawned by the Club of Rome to blunt and turn back industrial development. The Club of Rome's goals were to disseminate industrialization coupled with the spread of counterculture movements such as drugs, rock, sex, hedonism, Satanism and witchcraft. The Tavistock Institute, Stanford Research Institute and the Institute for Social Relations have delegates on the board of the Club of Rome and act as advisors for NATO to adopt the Aquarian Conspiracy. The Aquarian Conspiracy is an ideology to bring the masses together to embrace a new consciousness revolution otherwise known as the new world order, a one world religion.

The Club of Rome has its own private intelligence agency and has agents from David Rockefeller's INTERPOL. Every United States intelligence agency, the KGB and the Mossad work very closely with the Club of Rome. The only agency that remained beyond its reach is the East-German intelligence service otherwise known as the Ministry for State Security or the STASI. The Club of Rome has its own highly organized political and economic agencies. It was the Club of Rome who infiltrated Ronald Reagan's administration to retain the services of Paul Volcker, who was at the time the Chairman of the Federal Reserve. He was also another important member of the Committee of 300. At the time, Reagan wanted to dismiss Volcker, but Reagan broke his promise and kept him on. The Club of Rome, after playing a key role in the Cuban Missile Crisis, attempted to sell its "crisis management" under FEMA to President Kennedy. Several Tavistock scientists went to see the President to explain why it should be implemented, but the President Kennedy rejected the advice. Kennedy didn't want FEMA. The same year that Kennedy was murdered, Tavistock was back in Washington to talk with NASA. And this time the talks were successful. Tavistock was given a contract by NASA to evaluate the American public opinion on the effectiveness of the Space Program.

Henry Kissinger is an agent of The Club of Rome who was responsible for polarizing South America and the United States. He was responsible for overthrowing the Argentinian government through economic and political chaos alongside Lord Peter Carrington and had a direct hand in creating the 25-year war in El Salvador. El Salvador was chosen by the committee of 300 to turn Central America into a zone for a new Thirty-Year War, which task was allocated to Kissinger to carry out under the innocuous title of "The Andes Plan."

Kurt Lewin was an American German psychologist and worked closely with Tavistock, the Institute for Social Research, MIT and founded the National Training Laboratories. He was also the author of a work entitled "Time Perspective and Morale" which was a Club of Rome publication. Lewin, who was considered a pioneer of behavioral psychology, wrote about how to break down the morale of nations and individual leaders. Here is an excerpt from his publication: "One of the main techniques for breaking morale through a strategy of terror consists in exactly this tactic: keep the person hazy as to where he stands and just what he may expect. In addition, if frequent indecisions between severe disciplinary measures and promise of good treatment together with the spreading of contradictory news make the structure of the situation unclear, then the individual may cease to know whether a particular plan would lead toward or away from his goal. Under these conditions, even those individuals who have definite goals and are ready to take risks are paralyzed by the severe inner conflict in regard to what to do."

This Club of Rome blueprint applies not only to individuals but to countries as well, particularly the government leaders. The Club of Rome's plan is to demoralize the world so in the end we feel that we should follow or that we "deserve" what is coming. The sad part is most of the world is following the plan like sheep. According to Dr. John Coleman, any seemingly strong leader who appears to "rescue" the nation must be guarded as the most suspect. Remember it was Ruhollah Khomeini who was groomed by British intelligence for years, especially during his time in Paris, before he suddenly appeared as the savior of Iran.

The Club of Rome feels confident that it has carried out the Committee of 300's mandate to "ruin" the United States. After a centuries long of waging war on this nation, who will doubt their victory? Since the sixties the United States has been demoralized by drugs, rock and roll, pornography, sexual liberation, abortion and the complete decline of the family unit.

They have caused the worst depressions and economic collapses the world has ever seen. Destroying big cities, putting millions of people out of work, refusing to help our mentally disturbed veterans, and commits the ghastliest crimes against humanity.

Our country is seeing the worst homeless population in history, our government is populated with Jesuit agents at every level, corruption within our government and military has reached endemic proportions. It feels like the United States is at an epic decline and ready to collapse at any given moment.

The Club of Rome has succeeded in shutting down the Christian churches; it has succeeded in created an army of charismatic evangelicals who fight for the Zionist State of Israel. Dr. John Coleman once wrote, "During the Gulf War of genocide I received scores of letters asking me how I could oppose "a just Christian war against Iraq." How could I doubt that Christian fundamentalist support for the (Committee of 300's) war against Iraq was not Biblical-- after all didn't Billy Graham pray with President Bush just before the shooting started? Doesn't the Bible speak of "wars and rumors of wars?"

The Committee of 300 planned the first Club of Rome meeting in 1969 in the United States under the title "The Association of the Club of Rome." The Club of Rome created chapters in many nations across the world to keep pushing their global agendas. The next meeting was held in 1970 led by Thomas Berry and they titled it the "Riverdale Center of Religious Research." Thomas Berry was a professor of theology at the Jesuit university, Fordham. He was invited to teach at Fordham by Jesuit Christopher Mooney. Thomas was an expert on all world religions and philosophies, owned over 10,000 books and this made him the perfect contributor to the Club of Rome. The following year the Committee of 300 moved the conference to Houston, Texas which is referred to as "The Woodlands Conference." George Mitchell, who organized the meeting titled it "The Limits to Growth: The First Biennial Assessment of

Alternatives to Growth." Mitchell was the pioneer of fracking in Galveston, Texas. He was also a billionaire and huge supporter of sustainable development. Club of Rome meetings have been held in Houston ever since.

The First Global Conference on the Future was held in July of 1980 by Tavistock. Over 4000 social engineers and members of think tanks all operating under the Club of Rome umbrella organizations. This conference on the Future had the blessing of the White House which was called the "President's Commission for a National Agenda for the Eighties" where the president officially recommended the policies of the Club of Rome as a guide for United States policies. It was declared that the United States economy is moving out of the industrial phase, which echoed the voice of Zbigniew Brzezinski who was Jimmy Carter's senior advisor at the time. This provided more proof of the control exercised by the Committee of 300 over domestic and foreign affairs of the United States. It seems that everything is rigged against us and we are socially, politically and economically set up to remain locked in their control.

It is not difficult to see how the Club of Rome has maintained its secretive grip on all U.S. energy policies and the birth of environmentalism opposition to nuclear energy. The Club of Rome has done everything in their power to keep the United States from becoming a strong industrial nation. The effects of anti-nuclear policy of the Club of Rome can be measured in terms of rusted steel mills, closed shipyards and neglected railroads.

The Club of Rome's plan is to demoralize the world so in the end we feel defeated and apathetic. That we hate each other. That we "deserve" what is coming to us. Don't buy into it.

COMMITTEE OF 300

"How the Committee of 300 arranges elections is far from "fair and free" and it has no meaning in the United States. The candidates are selected by the Committee of 300 so it does matter who wins the election, for them."

The Committee of 300, who refer to themselves as the Olympians, do not hide who they are. In fact, they are in open view, in plain sight. These men and women are the servants of the New World Order, the one world government. They act like they are dutiful but are the exact opposite. The Committee of 300's goal is to return the world to the dark ages or even worse. They believe in a better, smaller world that has eliminated all of the useless eaters and consumers of the natural resources. They are against pro-creating and all about depopulating the planet. And one way they set forth to do this was to attack Christianity. The Black Nobility, Italy's deep state known as P2 Masonry and the Red Brigades (a left-wing socialist terrorist group) are all working towards the same goals.

These families desire to return to a feudal system where they are in complete control and will once again become the absolute rulers and I believe this is the real New World Order a one world government. Most of the Committee of 300's wealth arose out of the opium trade war with China and India. This group looks to create chaos and madness on a global scale, followed by depressions, to serve as psychological operations and techniques for bigger things to come, like what is going on right now, the great reset! It's been written that there are estimated 3-5,000 families that own and control the entire world's economy but the number of people who control them is even fewer. This cartel controls every aspect of the global economic network from banks, insurance companies, raw materials, transportation, factories, stocks, media, intelligence…and it is all coordinated by secret societies. That is their purpose.

In the beginning, Italy and Pakistan were the two primary targets of the Committee. Italy was a target due to its close European economic and political ties to the Middle East and home to the Catholic Church. In 1978,

Prime Minister of Italy, Aldo Moro severely opposed the depopulation agenda. Moro was kidnapped by the Red Brigades and murdered. During his trial some of the Red Brigade members testified that there was a plot involving people of the United States at the highest levels to take out Moro. IT's been written that the agent who originally threatened him was Henry Kissinger. Kissinger told Moro that if he didn't change is economic policy in Italy, he would severely pay for it. Moro was kidnapped, murdered and found in the trunk of a car.

Kissinger was and still is an agent of the Council on Foreign Relations, Club of Rome and the Royal Institute of Affairs. Kissinger's main role was to destabilize the United States through the Vietnam, Korean and Middle Eastern wars. He was also involved in the Gulf war to get Kuwait back under control and making an example out of Iraq so other small nations would not be tempted to try and create their own sovereignty. Kissinger also threatened the president of Pakistan, Ali Bhutto, because he favored nuclear weapons for the country. Nuclear power is hated all over the world and this superficial environmentalist agenda was established and financially supported by the Committee of 300 so small countries could become independent of US foreign aid. Nuclear generated electricity is key for these small countries to become sovereign.

The Committee of 300 pushes social change on a global scale, usually in the form of a depression and want people all over the world to be living in a welfare state. The Committee of 300 bases their ideologies from Felix Dzerzinski who saw mankind as nothing but cattle. During a 1967 meeting in France called the "Conference on Transatlantic Imbalance and Collaboration" the Committee of 300 decided that NASA needed to be stopped. They wanted the US to end its technological progress. It was also decided at this meeting that if they did not bring a one world government there would be total chaos in the future. They wanted all-natural resources to be allocated through global planning. The 1973 Israeli-Arab war was manifested on purpose to bring natural resources like petroleum under the control of the Committee of 300.

The Committee of 300 is a secret elite group that has inherited the beliefs of the cult of Isis, Illuminism, and Dionysius and refer to themselves as the Olympians because they truly believe they are equal in power to the

Gods such as Olympus and Lucifer. They believe they have the divine right to rule and they wrote 2 goals to implement to gain this control.

Here they are:

1. A One World Government-New World Order with a unified church and monetary system under their direction
2. The utter destruction of all national identity and national pride.
3. The destruction of Christianity
4. Control of each and every person through means of mind control
5. An end to all industrialization and the production of nuclear generated electric power
6. Legalization of drugs and pornography
7. Depopulation of large cities
8. Suppression of all scientific development
9. Inducing wars and starvation as they see fit and reduce the population by 100 million by 2050
10. Demoralize workers in the labor class by creating mass unemployment.
11. Implement FEMA
12. Infiltrate through Rock Music such as the Rolling Stones and Beatles
13. To strengthen the Zionist state
14. Spread Muslim brotherhood religious cults
15. To implement Jesuit Liberation Theology to undermine Christians
16. To cause a total collapse of the world's economies and create political chaos
17. To take control of all Foreign and domestic policies of the United States
18. Give full power to the United Nations, the International Monetary Fund, the Bank of International Settlements, the World Court
19. Penetrate and corrupt all governments
20. Organize a world-wide terrorist groups
21. Take control of education in America

The Committee of 300's Zbigniew Brzezinski published two books that he did not write himself, but they were the blueprints of the Committee of 300's plans. He wrote that by the end of the century the possibility of biochemical mind control and genetic tinkering with man could rise some difficult questions. Brzezinski is of Polish nobility, he was Jimmy Carter's senior advisor, he was a member of the Council on Foreign Relations and member of the Club of Rome and the Committee of 300. He promoted the use of LSD and the new world order. In 1981, the Committee of 300 warned every nation in the world, including Russia that there will be chaos unless the committee of 300 takes complete control for the New World Order. Control will be planned and executed through global planning and crisis management.

It is my belief that American has been brainwashed into thinking that socialism and communism is the biggest threat to our country. But it's not. The greatest danger comes from the huge number of traitors in our country. The constitution warned us about being watchful of the enemy within our gates. These enemies are servants of the Committee of 300 who have been placed in extremely high positions of power within our own government. The Aspen Institute of Colorado is one of the main assets in America under the Committee of 300. The Committee has done everything in their power to keep Mexico down, as a peasant country. A prosperous Mexico would only be a plus for America due to trading and exports of nuclear technology.

The Committee of 300 has been around for over 175 years but did not take its present form until 1897. The Committee is made of hundreds of think tanks and front organizations that oversee government leaders and private businesses. The Order of the Garter is the inner secret society within the Order of St. John of Jerusalem which is the British part of the Knights of Malta. Queen Elizabeth the second is known to be the head of this inner group. The Order of the Garter was founded during the reign of Edward the third and pretends to be a Christian organization. The Order of the Garter is also known as "The Foundation." Its purpose is to organize and implement plans for the Committee of 300. Its insignia has an eight-pointed star which derives from the Templars.

Its members include most if not all of the British Royal Family, other European nobility, the Rothschilds and a mix of other wealthy individuals scattered across Europe and America. The Order of the Garter is the parent organization over Freemasonry, world-wide. When a man becomes a 33rd degree Mason, he swears allegiance to the Order of the Garter.

Dr. John Coleman had access to intelligence agency secret documents that the thirteen bloodlines of the Illuminati (Astor, Bundy, Collins, DuPont, Freeman, Kennedy, Li, Onassis, Reynolds, Rockefeller, Rothschild, Russell, Van Duyn) have very intimate roles with the American and British intelligence cults. Many of these family members have worked and operated under the Committee of 300. It is very important to note that just because they are labeled "13 bloodlines of the Illuminati) does not make them supreme power. These American families were used. If the Kennedy family were so powerful, they would not have had so many tragedies in their ancestry. See what I'm saying? I believe the "13 bloodlines of the Illuminati" is a red herring a distraction to who the true power families are. You can read the book Bloodlines of the Illuminati on the CIA website. Now why would that be? The Astor's and Russell families profited the most from the China opium trade.

The Committee of 300 working with the Heritage Foundation placed socialists in every single position of power in the Reagan administration. Important members of the Committee of 300 are members of NATO and they have planted agents in the United States, Congress, the government, advisors to the President, secretary of state and ambassadors. And by 2021, you can see that everything is rigged against us. If we are to survive, we must release the stranglehold the Committee of 300 has over America.

In every election since Calvin Coolidge ran for the White House, the Committee of 300 has been able to plant its agents in key positions in government so that it matters not who gets the White House post. For example, every one of the candidates who ran for the Presidency, from the time of Franklin D. Roosevelt, were selected, some like to call it "hand-picked," by the Council on Foreign Relations acting on the instructions of the RIIA. Since 1980, every candidate has been handpicked by the Council on Foreign Relations. According to John Coleman, it is the American Secretary of State who is the conduit for communication, taking instructions from London and advising the president how to act.

The only way we can fight back is to expose these people for who they are and wake up the masses. But the problem is most people have issues with the idea of a global conspiracy. They have a hard time accepting a global conspiracy and especially the fact that our own government is corrupt. They want us confused. They want us brainwashed and mind controlled. But we can't fight against an unknown enemy. Knowing who our enemy is, is vital to surviving.

COUNCIL ON FOREIGN RELATIONS

"Most of us know, both the left and right of the political spectrum is controlled by the Council on Foreign Relations."

The Council on Foreign Relations was formally established in Paris in 1919 along with its British Counterpart the Royal Institute of International Affairs. The men who founded this group were Col. Edward Mandel House, Walter Lippmann, Herbert Hoover, Eustace Percy, Paul Warburg, Isaiah Bowman, James Shotwell, Allen Dulles, Christian Herter, Cary Coolidge and David Rockefeller. The Council on Foreign Relations and Royal Institute of International Affairs can trace their roots back to a secret organization founded and funded by Cecil Rhodes, who became fabulously wealthy by exploiting the people of South Africa. This is where the term "Rhodes scholar" derives.

The CFR has launched an international initiative to inject agendas and ideas into the public debate and control the leading institutions by tracking the decisions and policies of the G20. The G20 is an international forum for the governments and central banks from twenty countries around the world to discuss policies pertaining to financial stability. The members include Argentina, Australia, Brazil, Canada, China, European Union, France, Germany, India, Indonesia, Italy, Japan, Mexico, Russia, Saudi Arabia, South Africa, South Korea, Turkey, United Kingdom and the United States.

In addition to the annual conference the CFR provides an ongoing collaboration with its members to experiment with technology and responding to breaking crisis. There are two types of council memberships. The first one is "for life" and the second one is "term" which lasts for five years available to those who are between the ages of 30-36. To be nominated for life you must be seconded by a minimum of three members.

The CFR has only 3000 members, but they control over three-quarters of the nation's wealth. The CFR runs the state department and the CIA, and they have placed over 100 CFR members in every presidential administration since Woodrow Wilson. This group works to misinform and disinform the president to act in the best interest of the CFR, not the American people. The men and women are part of a "Secret Team" that play key parts in carrying out the psycho-political operations on behalf of the President. The "Secret Team" is set up as circles within circles. Not every Council member knows exactly what psycho-political operations are being planned or what their exact role in the operation is. This allows them to deny responsibility and deny Council sponsorship of the operation.

The Secret Team circles include Council on Foreign Relations members in top positions:

- Legislative, executive, and judicial branches of government
- Television, radio, and newspaper corporations
- Law firms
- Prestigious universities
- Private foundations
- Public corporations
- Think tanks and University Institutes
- Top commands in the military

Many men who you might recognize being part of this group were/are: Allen and John Dulles, David Rockefeller, Henry Kissinger, William Bundy, Zbigniew Brzezinski, Roger Ailes, Joe Biden, Madeleine Albright, Warren Beatty, Michael Bloomberg, Richard Branson, Tom Brokaw, Edgar Bronfman, George H.W. Bush, Dick Cheney, Bill and Hillary Clinton, George Clooney, Katie Couric, Mario Cuomo, David Geffen, Newt Gingrich, Angelina Jolie, Les Moonves, Rupert Murdoch, Sandra Day O'Connor, Pricilla Presley, Janet Reno, Dan Rather, Diane Sawyer, George Soros, George Stephanopoulos, Barbara Walters, Fareed Zakaria, Carl Sagan, Shirley Temple, and other people associated with Harvard, MIT, Morgan Stanley, Wall Street, Black Rock, Honeywell, the Washington Post and more.

One of its founders was Edward Mandell House who was Woodrow Wilson's chief advisor and rumored at the time to be the nation's real power from 1913-1921. On his watch the Federal Reserve Act passed in December of 1913 while all the Americans were home for Christmas and distracted. This act gave money creation power to bankers and the 16th amendment was ratified that following February, creating the federal income tax to provide a revenue stream to pay for government debt service.

From the beginning the Council on Foreign Relations was committed to "a one world government based on a centralized global financing system." Today the Council on Foreign Relations is strongest in the United States and has thousands of influential members, including people in the corporate media. They keep a very low profile like many of these groups of the Round Table, especially in regard to their real agenda.

Presidents (Eisenhower, Ford, Carter, Bush and Clinton) were CFR members. The Supreme Court has been packed with CFR insiders. The CFR's British counterpart is the Royal Institute of International Affairs and these groups profit by creating tension and hate. Their target is British and American citizens. The CFR specializes in psychological operations. In 1947 Council on Foreign Relations members George Kennan, Walter Lippmann, Paul Nitze, Dean Achenson, and Walter Krock took part in a psycho-political operation forcing the Marshall Plan on the American public. The psychological operation included an "anonymous" letter credited to a Mr. X, which appeared in the Council on Foreign Relations magazine FOREIGN AFFAIRS. The letter opened the door for the CFR controlled Truman administration to take a hard line against the threat of Soviet expansion.

Arthur Schlesinger, Jr., a historian called the CFR "a front organization for the heart of the American establishment." The group meets privately and only publishes what it wishes the public to know. Its members are only Americans. Past and current members of the Council on Foreign relations are nearly all presidential candidates of both parties, leading senators and congressmen, key members of the fourth estate and their bosses and top officials of the FBI, CIA, NSA, department of defense and other leading government members of top government. Agencies.

Since 1921, the Council on Foreign Relation's power and agenda have been unchanged, and they serve as the virtual employment agency for the federal government under both Democrats and Republicans. It advocates a global superstate with America and other nations by sacrificing their sovereignty and central power. A Council on Foreign Relations member and founder, Paul Warburg was a member of Roosevelt's brain trust. His son, James, told the Senate Foreign Relations Committee in 1950, "We shall have world government whether or not you like it; by conquest or consent."

The Council on Foreign Relations planned a New World Order before 1942 and they drafted the original United Nations proposal, presented it to Franklin Roosevelt who announced it publicly the next day. In 1945, the Council on Foreign Relations members comprised of over 40 of the United States delegates. According to Professor G. William Domhoff, the author of Who Rules America, the Council on Foreign Relations operates in "small groups of about 25, who bring together leaders from the six conspirator categories (industrialists, financiers, ideologues, military, professional specialists such as lawyers and doctors and organized labor) for detailed discussions of specific topics in the area of foreign affairs." Domhoff also said, "The Council on Foreign Relations, while not financed by government, works so closely with it that it is difficult to distinguish Council action simulated by government from autonomous actions. (Its) most important sources of income are leading corporations and major foundations." Three of the most powerful are the Carnegie, Rockefeller and Ford foundations.

The Council on Foreign Relations have a stranglehold on the United States government cabinet members. The National Security Act of 1947 established the office of Secretary of Defense. Since then, over 15 department of defense secretaries have been CFR members. Since 1940, every secretary of state, except James Byrnes has been a Council on Foreign Relations member and/or Trilateral Commission member or both. For the past 80 years, virtually every key United States National Security and Foreign Policy Advisor has been a Council on Foreign Relations member. Nearly all top generals and admirals have been Council on Foreign Relations members. Many presidential candidates were/are

CFR members including Herbert Hoover, Adlai Stevenson, Dwight Eisenhower, John F Kennedy, Richard Nixon, Gerald Ford, Jimmy Carter (also a member of Trilateral Commission), George H.W. Bush, Bill Clinton, John Kerry, John McCain

Numerous CIA directors were/are CFR members including Richard Helmes, James Schlesinger, William Casey, William Webster, Robert Gates, John Deutsch, James Woolsey, George Tenet, Porter Goss, Michael Hayden and Leon Panetta. You can also find members of the United States Supreme Court in this list including Ruth Bader Ginsberg. The Council on Foreign Relation's "special group/secret team" vets them for acceptability. Presidents are told who to appoint including members of the high court.

Many treasury secretaries were/are members including George Schultz, William Simon, Lloyd Bentsen, Douglas Dillon, James Baker, Nicholas Brady, Robert Rubin, Henry Paulson and Tim Geithner.

Hadley Cantril wrote a book in 1967 called, The Human Dimension: Experiences in Policy Research and wrote: "government psycho-political operations are propaganda campaigns designed to create perpetual tension and to manipulate different groups of people to accept the particular climate and opinion the Council on Foreign Relation seeks to achieve the world." Ken Adachi, a Canadian writer once wrote, "What most Americans believe to be public opinion is in reality carefully crafted and scripted propaganda designed to elicit a desired behavioral response from the public." Alex Carey, an Australian academic wrote, "The growth of democracy, the growth of corporate power and the growth of corporate propaganda is a means of protecting corporate power against democracy."

Think tanks in America are no different and serve the same purpose. Numerous think tanks are staffed with CFR members. Most of its life members also belong to the Trilateral Commission and Bilderberg Group where they operate in secret and hold all the power over the United States and world affairs. The Council on Foreign Relations has a tight grasp on media control. They believe the Council on Foreign Relations leadership must "make an end run around national sovereignty, eroding it piece by piece, until the very notion disappears from public discourse."

In February of 1941, the CFR officially became part of the State Department. This established the "Division of Special Research" run by Nazis in America. And they are still here. Their main goal was to create psychological operations throughout the world to push their psychotic agendas. Some of these were the Marshall Plan, Cold War, NSC-68, to name a few.

In 1943, the OSS released a top-secret document claiming that Fascist members of the Council on Foreign Relations infiltrated Hitler's Nazi party to bring him more power and to justify the World War. The report calls Hitler "glib" and "amateur".

Walter Lippmann was an American writer, reporter and political commentator, famous for first introducing the concept of the cold war, coined the term "stereotype" and wrote a book in 1922 titled, Public Opinion. Lippmann was close ally to the CFR and helped enable political psychological operations on the American people. In his book, Lippmann paints a graphic picture of what a society controlled by an "independent, expert organization" would look like. A society controlled by an "independent, expert organization," arranging chains of bondage from childhood by corrupting the societies knowledge base, and deciding what shadows to project on the wall, would be a society of prisoners that couldn't use their heads to act in their own best interest. They would become a society of slaves living in a realm of fear. Lippmann advocated for the CFR heavily.

Foundations are used by The Council on Foreign Relations to funnel corporate and personal wealth into the policy-making process. Foundations are tax-free. Contributions to foundations are deductible from federal corporate and individual income taxes. The Foundations themselves are not subject to federal income taxation. Foundations control hundreds of Billions of dollars of money that would normally go to pay federal and individual income taxes. George Soros is one of the world's richest men (estimated net worth is ten billion) and arguably the biggest international investor in history. Soros uses the money he steals to fund a group of international foundations some of them are:

- Ford Foundation
- Lilly Foundation
- Rockefeller Foundation
- Duke Endowment
- Kresge Foundation
- Kellogg Foundation
- Mott Foundation
- Pew Mutual Trust
- Hartford Foundation
- Alfred P. Sloan Foundation
- Carnegie Foundation

The CFR controls the US banking industry and has controlled the Federal Reserve since its inception. Many of the members at the Federal Reserve are also CFR members. Since 2020, the CFR is focused on diversity, cybersecurity, climate change dealing with the coronavirus and the Biden/Harris transition.

I have said this time and time again. The only way to stop these people are by making them known to the public. Tell other Americans who these groups are, what they are doing and write your elected representatives and demand they investigate their shady actions.

TRILATERAL COMMISSION

"Shortly, the public will be unable to reason or think for themselves. They'll only be able to parrot the information they've been given on the previous night's news."

The Trilateral Commission was founded by David Rockefeller in July of 1973 and is composed of approximately 390 elites in business, banking, and politics. The purpose of the group is to foster cooperation between Japan, Western Europe and North America. Other founding members were Zbigniew Brzenzski, Alan Greenspan and Paul Volcker both heads of the Federal Reserve. Jeffrey Epstein was also a notable member.

At the first meeting in Tokyo, they shared four goals which all centered around globalization in other words, a New World Order. According to Alex Christopher, author of Pandora's Box, "The Trilateral Commission is an international organization founded by David Rockefeller who also had a part in the founding of the Council on Foreign Relations, Inc., and who is the chairman of the board. The Trilateral Commission is the illuminati's attempt to unite Western Europe's common market, Japan, Canada and the United States into an economic and political confederacy. What they couldn't do through the political side of the Illuminati (Council on Foreign Relations) they are trying now through the economic approach."

According to Anthony Sutton and Patrick M. Wood, "The Trilateral Commission was founded by the persistent maneuvering of David Rockefeller and Zbigniew Brzezinski. Rockefeller, [then] chairman of the ultra-powerful Chase Manhattan Bank, a director of many major multinational corporations and 'endowment funds' has long been a central figure in the mysterious Council on Foreign Relations. Brzezinski, a brilliant prognosticator of one world idealism, has been a professor at Columbia University and the author of several books that have served as 'policy guidelines' for the CFR. Brzezinski served as the (Trilateral) commission's executive director from its inception in 1973 until late 1976 when he was appointed by President Carter as assistant to the president for national security affairs."

From the 1979 book With No Apologies by Barry Goldwater it states that "David Rockefeller's newest international cabal [the Trilateral Commission] ... is intended to be the vehicle for multinational consolidation of the commercial and banking interests by seizing control of the political government of the United States. The Trilateral Commission represents a skillful, coordinated effort to seize control and consolidate the four centers of power — political, monetary, intellectual, and ecclesiastical. All this is to be done in the interest of creating a more peaceful, more productive world community. What the Trilaterals' truly intend is the creation of a worldwide economic power superior to the political governments of the nation-states involved. They believe the abundant materialism they propose to create will overwhelm existing differences. As managers and creators of the system they will rule the future."

The Trilateral Commission is propped up as a unified economic cooperation but in reality, is another front to bring in a one world currency and world governance. They are working to set up a framework that is necessary for banks and corporations to assume global control.

According to Laurie Strand, "Many of the original members of the Trilateral Commission are now in positions of power where they are able to implement policy recommendations of the Commission; recommendations that they, themselves, prepared on behalf of the Commission. It is for this reason that the Commission has acquired a reputation for being the Shadow Government of the West ...The Trilateral Commission's tentacles have reached so far in the political and economic sphere that it has been described by some as a cabal of powerful men out to control the world by creating a supernational community dominated by the multinational corporations."

Notable members of the trilateral commission are: Henry Kissinger, David Gergen, Madeleine Albright, Dick and Lynn Cheney, George H.W. Bush, Jimmy Carter, Al Gore, Bill Clinton, Diane Feinstein and other political figures. There are numerous banking institutions that are represented at these meetings and they are European Central Bank, World Bank, IMF, the Federal Reserve, Chase Morgan, Citibank, Bank of America, Bank One, Bank of Tokyo, Bank of Japan and more.

Fuji Xerox, Goldman Sachs, AIG, ExxonMobil, Shell, Chevron, Texaco, Sony, Samsung, Comcast, Time Warner, Carlyle Group, Levi-Strauss, Daikin, Sara Lee, GE, GM, Ford, Chrysler, Toyota, Mitsubishi, Johnson and Johnson, IBM, Boeing, and Citigroup are among the corporations that are owned by the Trilateral Commission.

"In 1984 I warned of a takeover of world governments being orchestrated by these people. There was an obvious plan to subvert true democracies and selected leaders were not being chosen based upon character but upon their loyalty to an economic system run by the elites and dedicated to preserving their power. All we have now are pseudo democracies." – Dr. Johannes Koeppl

The Trilateral Commission is the driver behind the technocracy, 5G and smart cities. They have been driving modern technology since the 70's. According to William Cooper, the Trilateral Commission's logo is the trilateral insignia which derives from the alien flag known as the "Trilateral Insignia". Many of their operative work for Social Media companies either leading them or sitting on the boards. The following think tanks have been linked under the Trilateral Commission:

- Aspen Institute
- Brookings Institution
- Center for Defense Information
- Columbia University
- Ford Foundation
- Georgetown University
- Harvard University
- Hoover Institute
- Hudson Institute
- MIT
- Rand Corporation
- Rockefeller Foundation
- World Watch Institute

The following media companies are linked to the Trilateral Commission:

- CBS
- Los Angeles Times
- Time
- Foreign Policy Magazine
- Chicago Sun-Times
- CNN
- Washington Post

Every institution under the guise of "world peace" is easily working to achieve the one world government. The Trilateral Commission is very similar to the Bilderberg group meaning that it is funded by the Rockefeller empire but what makes it unique is that it brought the Japanese ruling elite into the inner councils of the global power brokers and helped increase Japan's growing influence in the economic and political arena.

Their goal every four years is to place a Trilateral-influence president in the White House or be able to groom a candidate who would be willing to cooperate with the Trilateral's aims.

ROYAL INSTITUTE OF INTERNATIONAL AFFAIRS

"One of the most important secret societies of the 20th century is called the Round Table. It is based in Britain with branches across the world. It is the Round Table that ultimately orchestrates the network of the Bilderberg Group, Council on Foreign Relations, Trilateral Commission and the Royal Institute of International Affairs."

The Royal Institute of International Affairs (RIAA or Chatham House) is a think tank headquartered in London. It was founded in 1920 by Lionel Curtis, although this fact was concealed for many years and he was presented to the public as merely one among a number of founders. It has been written that the institute was founded by the Milner Group and it is said that this group still controls the group to this day. This institution was financially backed by Sir Abe Bailey.

World Leaders at the 1919 Paris Peace Conference

It is important to note the other benefactors of the Institute. In 1926, Carnegie, the Bank of England and the Rockefellers were the first. In 1929 many pledges and donations were made by some of the biggest banks and corporations, promising future grants to the Institute. These groups were:

- Anglo-Iranian Oil Company
- Bank of England
- Barclay's Bank
- Baring Brothers
- British American Tobacco Company
- British South Africa Company
- Central Mining and Investment Corporation
- Erlanger's, Ltd
- Ford Motor Company
- Hambros' Bank
- Imperial Chemical Industries
- Lazard Brothers
- Lever Brothers
- Lloyd's
- Lloyd's Ban
- Mercantile and General Insurance Company
- Midland Bank
- Reuters
- Rothschild and Sons
- Stern Brothers
- Vickers-Armstrong
- Westminster Bank
- Whitehall Securities Corporation

This group is headquartered in London and its mission is to provide authoritative commentary on world events and offer solutions to global challenges.

The Paris Peace Conference on May 30th, 1919 was held for the victorious allies of World War One to set peace terms for the defeated central powers (German, Austria, Ottoman Empire, Bulgaria). The conference involved diplomats from 32 countries and nationalities and its major decisions were the creation of the League of Nations. The League of Nation's main goals were to prevent human and drug trafficking, arms trades, global health and prisoners of war. Of course, it was infiltrated, like all great things.

Lionel Curtis had long been an advocate for the scientific study of international affairs and, following the beneficial exchange of information after the peace conference, argued that the method of expert analysis and debate should be continued when the delegates returned home in the form of international institute. Ultimately, what happened is, the British and American delegates formed separate institutes, with the Americans developing the Council on Foreign Relations in New York and the British developed the Royal Institute of International Affairs. These became two of the most secretive and powerful groups in the world.

The American group of experts, "the Inquiry," was dominated by special persons from institutions, Universities and dominated by J.P. Morgan and Company. This was not a coincidence. The Milner Group always had very close relationships with the associates of J.P. Morgan and with the various branches of the Carnegie Trust. These relationships, which are merely examples of the closely knit ramifications of international financial capitalism, were probably based on the financial holdings controlled by the Milner Group through the Rhodes Trust.

This group drew up a constitution and made a list of prospective members. Lionel Curtis and Gathorne-Hardy drew up the by-laws. No complete record exists of the meetings before the fall of 1921, but, beginning then, the principal speech at each meeting and resumes of the comments from the floor were published in the Journal:

1. At the first of these recorded meetings, D.G. Hogarth spoke on "The Arab States," with Lord Chelmsford in the chair. Stanley Reed, Chirol, and Meston spoke from the floor.
2. Two weeks later, H.A.L. Fisher spoke on "The Second Assembly of the League of Nations," with Lord Robert Cecil in the chair. Temperley and Wilson Harris also spoke.
3. In November, Philip Kerr was the chief figure for two evenings on "Pacific Problems as They Would Be submitted to the Washington Conference."
4. At the end of the same month, A.J. Toynbee spoke on "The Greco-Turkish Question," with Sir Arthur Evans in the chair,

5. Early in December his father-in-law, Gilbert Murray, spoke on "Self-Determination," with Lord Sumner in the chair.
6. In January 1922, Chaim Weizmann spoke on "Zionism".
7. In February, Chirol spoke on "Egypt".
8. In April, Walter T. Layton spoke on "The Financial Achievement of the League of Nations," with Lord Robert Cecil in the chair.
9. In June, Wilson Harris spoke on "The Genoa Conference," with Robert H. Brand in the chair.
10. In October, Ormsby-Gore spoke on "Mandates," with Lord Lugard in the chair.
11. Two weeks later, Sir Arthur Steel-Maitland spoke on "The League of Nations," with H.A.L. Fisher in the chair.
12. In March 1923, Harold Butler spoke on the "International Labor Office," with G.N. Barnes in the chair.
13. Two weeks later, Philip Kerr spoke on "The Political Situation in the United States," with Arthur Balfour in the chair.
14. In October 1923, Edward F.L. Wood (Lord Halifax) spoke on "The League of Nations," with H.A.L. Fisher in the chair.
15. In November 1924, E.R. Peacock (Parkin's protege) spoke on "Mexico," with Lord Eustace Percy in the chair.
16. In October 1925, Leopold Amery spoke on "The League of Nations," with Robert Cecil as chairman,
17. In May 1926, H.A.L. Fisher spoke on the same subject, with Neill Malcolm as chairman.
18. In November 1925, Paul Mantoux spoke on "The Procedure of the League," with Brand as chairman.
19. In June 1923, Edward Grigg spoke on "Egypt," with D.G. Hogarth in the chair.

These rather scattered observations will show how the meetings were peppered by members of the Milner Group. This does not mean that the Group monopolized the meetings, or even spoke at a majority of them. The point is these meetings were controlled by the Milner Group. The meetings generally took place once a week from October to June of each year, and probably members of the Group spoke or presided at no more than a quarter of them. This, however, represents far more than their due proportion, for when the Institute had 2500, members the Milner Group amounted to no more than 100.

The proceedings of the meetings were generally printed in abbreviated form in the Journal of the Institute. Until January 1927, this periodical was available only to members, but since that date it has been open to public subscription. The first issue was as anonymous as the first issue of The Round Table: no list of editors, no address, and no signature to the opening editorial introducing the new journal.

Jerome Greene was an international banker close to the Milner Group. Originally Mr. Greene had been a close associate of J.D. Rockefeller but in 1917 he shifted to the international banking firm Lee, Higginson, and Company of Boston. He became a resident of Toynbee Hall and established a relationship with the Milner Group. Greene was a trustee and secretary of the Rockefeller Foundation in 1913-1917 and was a trustee of the Rockefeller Institute and of the Rockefeller General Education Board in 1912-1939. It must be pointed out that the majority of the study groups of the RIIA are direct descendants of the roundtable meetings of the original Round Table group.

They have been defined by Stephen King-Hall as, "unofficial Royal Commissions charged by the Council of Chatham House with the investigation of specific problems." These study groups are generally made up of persons who are not members of the Milner Group, and their reports are frequently published by the Institute. In 1932 the Rockefeller Foundation gave the Institute a grant of $8000 a year for five years to advance the study-group method of research. Why would they do that? This grant was extended for five years more in 1937. Without much substantial evidence it is easy to see that the RIIA was and still is funded by the Milner/Rockefeller alliance.

In general, the funds came from the various endowments, banks, and industrial concerns with which the Milner Group had relationships. The original money in the early 1900's came from Abe Bailey. When Sir Abe died in 1940, the annual Report of the Council said, "With the passing of

Sir Bailey the Council and all the members of Chatham House mourn the loss of their most munificent Founder."

In 1929 pledges were obtained from important banks and corporations, promising annual grants to the Institute. Most of these had one or more members of the Milner Group on their boards of directors. Among some of the pledges were Anglo-Iranian Oil company, Bank of England, Barclay's Bank, Ford Motor Company, Hambros Bank, Midland Bank, Reuters, Rothschild and Sons, and Vickers Armstrong. The Astor family (13 bloodlines of the Illuminati) was also a generous donor.

It is important to note that Royal Institute of International Affairs had been researching potential post-war issues as early as 1939 through the Committee on Reconstruction. Whilst a number of staff returned to the Institute at the end of the war, a proportion of members found themselves joining a range of international organizations, including the United Nations and the International Monetary Fund.

The Royal Institute of International Affairs and the Council on Foreign Relations has always been loaded with partners, associates and employees of J.P. Morgan. The RIIA was able to extend its intellectual influence into countries outside the Commonwealth. This was done, for example, through the Intellectual Cooperation Organization of the League of Nations.

These were called the International Studies Conferences and devoted themselves to an effort to obtain different national points of view on international problems. The members of the Studies Conferences were twenty-five organizations. Twenty of these were Coordinating Committees created for the purpose in twenty different countries. The other five were the following organizations the Academy of International Law, the European Center of the Carnegie Endowment for International Peace, the Geneva School of International Studies, the Graduate Institute of International Studies at Geneva and the Institute of Pacific Relations. In two of these five, the influence of the Milner Group and its close allies was important.

The influence of the Group was decisive in the Coordinating Committees within the British Commonwealth, especially in the British Coordinating Committee for International Studies. The members of this committee were named by four agencies, three of which were controlled by the Milner Group. These groups were the London School of Economics and Political Science, the Department of International Politics at the University of Wales and the Montague Burton Chair of International Relations at Oxford. Four of the seven board members were members of the Milner group.

This brief portrait of the Royal Institute of International Affairs is to show that the Milner Group controls the Institute. Once you see the stranglehold this group has, the picture changes. The illusion is gone. This group has been controlled by the Milner Group since its inception.

The influence on research and study of the Royal Institute of International Affairs does not have the influence of an autonomous body but it is merely the instrument of another power. When you begin to realize that education, news and media are shaped by these think tanks you must understand who is shaping them. The Royal Institute of International Affairs is scary because whatever the goals this group had or will have, they are being completely controlled by a very small group.

No organization, think tank, group or country should allow what the Milner Group accomplished in Britain. These men used money and influence to shift their power and have complete control over publications, documenting their meetings, their actions and shaped public opinion to monopolize history. When it was decided that a super-power would control European affairs the Royal Institute of International Affairs founded the Tavistock Institute, which in turn created the North Atlantic Treaty Organization (NATO).

FEDERAL RESERVE

"It is well enough that people of the nation do not understand our banking and monetary system, for if they did, I believe there would be a revolution before tomorrow morning."

In 1886 a group of East Coast Millionaires including William Rockefeller, Joseph Pulitzer, J.P. Morgan, Henry Goodyear, and Edwin and George Gould bought Jekyll Island, Georgia, for $125,000. They named themselves the Jekyll Island Club. The activities of some of the members changed world events through orchestrated psychological operations and by the early 20th century the Jekyll Island Club represented 1/6th of the entire world's wealth.

On March 13, 1907 a financial panic was triggered by rumors that the Knickerbocker Bank, and The Trust Company of America were about to become insolvent. The rumors were started by the House of Morgan. There was a run on the banks. Morgan helped to avert the panic he helped to create. Morgan imported $100 million worth of gold from Europe to stop the run on the banks. This exercise was a Round Table psycho-political operation. It provided America with the perception and rationalization that what the United States needed was a central banking system.

The Senate created the National Monetary Commission to study the problem. Senator Nelson Aldrich (John D. Rockefeller's father-in-law) headed the commission. To investigate the matter the Commission toured the continent of Europe to study the European central banking system. Aldrich didn't have any banking experience. It took nearly two years and $300,000 of tax-payer money to wine and dine the men of the European central banking system before the committee was able to complete their study. Towards the end of 1910, a group of men held a secretive meeting on Jekyll Island, Georgia.

The purpose of the 1910 Jekyll Island meeting was to write the final recommendations for the National Monetary Commission report. Senator Aldrich arranged the meeting. The men who attended included:

- Henry P. Davison (House of Morgan - J.P. Morgan and Co.)
- Benjamin Strong (House of Morgan - Bankers Trust Co.)
- Frank A. Vanderlip (House of Rockefeller - National City Bank)
- A. Piatt Andres (Assistant Secretary of the Treasury)
- Paul Warburg (House of Warburg and House of Kuhn-Lobe & Co.)

According to the memoirs of Frank Vanderlip, "Despite my views about the value to society of greater publicity for the affairs of corporations, there was an occasion, near the close of 1910, when I was as secretive - indeed as furtive - as any conspirator... I do not feel it is any exaggeration to speak of our secret expedition to Jekyll Island as the occasion of the actual conception of what eventually became the **Federal Reserve System**."

Congress acted on the report and created the Federal Reserve act which President Woodrow Wilson signed in December of 1913 while Americans were preoccupied with Christmas and while no one was paying attention.

A small group of Americans, the Council on Foreign Relations, was using psychological warfare techniques not only as a means of systematic nationalistic aggression, but as a means of deceiving their own countrymen. In December of 1963, they published a book title, "The Federal Reserve System: Purposes and Functions" which was intended to persuade Americans to accept the massive control the Federal Reserve had over the American economy.

In the book we learn:

- The Federal Reserve is a corporation, accountable to the United States government, but owned by banks which have purchased shares of stock.

- The Federal Reserve Bank is the banker's banker. If a commercial or savings bank wants to lend more money to customers, it borrows money from its bank (Federal Reserve)
- The Federal Reserve is a watchdog that audits every banks records to make sure loan decisions are based on sound judgments and that regulations are being followed
- The Federal Reserve is the controller of the currency, the U.S. Governments bank where the Treasury has its bank account
- The Federal Reserve is the nation's check-clearing system - processing over 15 billion checks a year
- The Federal Reserve is the keeper of the world's gold
- The gold is kept in a vault at the New York Federal Reserve bank
- Most of the gold stored in the Fed belongs to other nations and represents about one-third of the official gold reserves of the world's non-communist countries

The Federal Reserve is run by a seven-member board of Governors appointed by the President and confirmed by the Senate. Terms of office last 14 years to insulate governors from political pressures. Terms are staggered, with one expiring every two years. There's one chairman and one vice-chairman, both of whom hold terms of four years. The seven members of the board of Governors, the President of the Federal Reserve Bank of New York, and four other Federal Reserve Bank Presidents are members of a group called the Federal Open Market Committee. This Committee is responsible for the purchase and sale of government securities. That means they are responsible for influencing the cost and availability of money and credit.

It is interesting to note that there is no mention of the Council on Foreign Relation's role in establishing and controlling the Federal Reserve System. While long terms on the board of governors were established to insulate governors from political pressures no safeguards were established to insulate governors from pressures from a private group such as the Council on Foreign Relations.

"They who control the credit of a nation direct the policy of governments and hold in their hands the destiny of the people." – Reginald McKenna

Midland Bank was established by the head of the Round Table, Lord Alfred Milner. Reginald McKenna served as the Chairman of the bank. According to historian, Carroll Quigley, the aim of the dynastic banking houses was, "...nothing less than to create a world system of financial control in private hands able to dominate the political system of each country and the economy of the world as a whole. This system was to be controlled in a feudalist fashion by the central banks of the world acting in concert, by secret agreements arrived at in frequent private meetings and conferences. The apex of the system was to be the Bank for International Settlements in Basle, Switzerland, a private bank owned and controlled by the world's central banks which were themselves private corporations. Each central bank in the hands of these men sought to dominate its government by its ability to control Treasury loans, to manipulate foreign exchanges, to influence the level of economic activity in the country, and to influence cooperative politicians by subsequent economic rewards in the business world."

Alan Greenspan, Paul Volcker, G. William Miller, and William McChesney Martin have all chaired the Federal Reserve board. All were members of the Council on Foreign Relations. The current chairman of the Federal Reserve is Jay Powell, and his term ends in 2028. He was nominated to the Federal Reserve by Donald Trump. He is a Jesuit, worked under George H.W. Bush and is a partner of the George Soros Carlyle Group.

In 1987 leaders of America's major banks went to Tokyo. They met with our finance minister and governor of the central bank. They urged more positive cooperation by Japanese banks. The big American banks were caught in the dilemma of their Latin American Debt. On the one hand, they had to suffer the losses caused in part by their own over-lending, which meant they could not continue being exposed to new loans to Latin America. On the other hand, they were unable to jettison Latin America, which for them was an important market. The leaders of the banks attending the meeting were:

- John Reed of Citibank
- Willard Butcher of Chase
- Lewis Preston of Morgan

- Tom Clausen of the Bank of America
- Reed, Butcher and Preston of the CFR

All of these men were members of the Council on Foreign Relations.

The United States Code contains the general and permanent laws of the United States. The United States Code is prepared and published by the Office of the Law Revision Counsel of the House of Representatives. The laws have been classified into fifty categories. A Category is called a Title. For example, laws pertaining to the President are found in Title 3 "The President." Title 12 is called "Banks and Banking." A reading of laws contained in Title 12 back up the statement that Congress has not given authority for determining money policy to the Federal Reserve System.

Title 50 "War and National Defense" spells out a role for the Federal Reserve. Title 50 Section 101 is the "National Security Emergency Preparedness Policy." In this policy, Part 15 reads:

- "the Secretary of the Treasury shall:
    - (1) Develop plans to maintain stable economic conditions and a market economy during national security emergencies; emphasize measures to minimize inflation and disruptions; and minimize reliance on direct controls of the monetary, credit, and financial systems. These plans will include provisions for:
        - (a) Increasing capabilities to minimize economic dislocations by carrying out appropriate fiscal, monetary, and regulatory policies and reducing susceptibility to manipulated economic pressures
        - (b) Providing the Federal Government with efficient and equitable financing sources and payment mechanisms"

Has the Federal Reserve been acting as if we have been in a perpetual National Security Emergency? Is the destiny of the American people being controlled by a group who have and hold the power to direct the credit policy of our nation? It would seem like it is.

Has it ever occurred to you that the federal government has no need of taxes for revenue? Are you aware that banks prefer lending to governments because governments seldom repay loans? Do you realize that if all debts, both public and private, were paid, there would be no money in circulation, at all?

These are only a few of the startling facts involving The Federal Reserve System. The Federal Reserve system intentionally disarms its victims. They are convinced that the subject of money and banking is far too complicated for the average person to understand it makes us all victims trapped in a world view that leaves us completely unable to live in true financial reality. We are controlled by money manipulators who are exploiting our ignorance for the advancement of their own despicable plans.

The most ironic fact about the Federal Reserve System is that it actually has NO RESERVES, and it is NOT A BANK! It exists only to make the rich richer. The act of borrowing money from the federal government causes money to spring into existence. Did you know that treasury IOUs (bonds) are converted by the Federal Reserve into money through the issuance of Federal Reserve checks with no actual money to cover them? This is completely and utterly illegal, but the United States congress made this legal because it allows our congressmen to take advantage of unlimited revenue without having to visibly "raise taxes."

To explain this in layman's terms, Federal Reserve checks are endorsed by the United States government and deposited into the Federal Reserve bank to pay off government expenses. This "money" creates the first wave of fiat (unbacked paper) that floods the economy. Commercial banks also create money out of nothing and collect interest on it (multiplying every dollar, over time). Without realizing it, Americans are paying federal income tax and this hidden tax which equals ten times the national debt. The ignorance of the American people is only due to disinformation. We are not taught about the financial system. We are not taught about the deception of inflation. These insiders are completely protected and their scam lives on. Since 1913, money in America had depreciated by over 1,000 percent.

Another sad and depressing fact is how the Federal Reserve protects and enriches international banks. Megabanks like Chase, Bank of America and Citicorp will lend third world countries loans knowing they will not be repaid, and they actually prefer this. Remember, they make their money on interest, not repayment.

> *"The right to issue fiat money would be as alarming as the mark of the beast in Revelation."* – George Reed

The Federal Reserve is the fourth central bank the United States has had, the previous three having crashed in inevitable raging inflation and widespread economic disaster. So clearly did our Founders understand and fear worthless paper money forced on the public by legal tender laws (precisely what we now have) that they filled the proceedings of the Constitutional Convention with statements of their horror of it. Americans today are deprived of the truth.

> *"I would rather reject the whole Constitution than grant the new government the right to issue fiat money."*
> – John Langdon

The International Monetary Fund/World Bank is already working in conjunction with the Federal Reserve as a world central bank. It has been written there is a world currency, already designed, awaiting a crisis to justify its introduction. From this point on, there will be no escape from the new world order. The name of the game is to spend on anything at any time. Their object is to bring down the system.

The war started in 2020 with the coronavirus scamdemic. War is used to make the people put up with all kinds of privation, taxation, and controls without complaint. It is created to deprive us of our God-given freedoms. No amount of sacrifice in the name of victory is rejected. Resistance is viewed as treason when in fact the "elected" officials are the guilty party of treasonous acts.

It is possible the Federal Reserve can be abolished, the national debt paid, and the country returned to a solid monetary system based on silver and gold. All that is needed are the efforts of concerned and caring

Americans. We can free ourselves from the one-world conspirators. It can be done.

"I am a most unhappy man. I have unwittingly ruined my country. A great industrial nation is now controlled by the system of credit." – Woodrow Wilson

TAVISTOCK

"If you don't learn to control your mind, someone else will."

Our Tavistock story begins in the late 1880's with Arthur Cherep-Spiridovich, a white Russian loyalist, who was anti-communist. He was a Russian general and claimed to be well-versed in international affairs and predicted huge world events. In 1902 he warned Kings and Dukes about future assassination attempts. He was right. He also predicted the first world war due to his knowledge about "the hidden hand", in which he called, a secret group of 300 Jewish families, controlling the world events. Spiridovich emigrated to New York and wrote the book "Secret World Government." He was found dead in his hotel room, in 1926, at the age of 59, from suicide.

So, who was this secret group of Jews? Spiridovich was talking about the Committee of 300. Walter Rathenau, a German politician, once stated, "Three hundred men, all of whom know one another, guide the economic destinies of the Continent and seek their successors from within their own environment."

Dr. John Coleman was a British intelligence officer who gained access to a private British museum in London. It was here that Coleman discovered the highly classified documents of Tavistock. It angered him so much he spent five years reading and deciphering them and wrote the book *The Tavistock Institution of Human Relations: Shaping the moral, Spiritual, Cultural, Political and Economic Decline of the Unites States of America*.

Tavistock was secretly started in 1913, and was funded by the British monarchy, the Milner Group, the Rockefellers and the Rothschilds. Tavistock's first purpose was to create propaganda to start a war between Britain and Germany. The motivation behind the war was inspired by Germany's rapid progress on surpassing Britain with economic power. Tavistock's second purpose was to infiltrate America by establishing a centralized bank, removing the gold standard and the degradation of women and religion. This group's mission was to establish a complete breakdown of America's values to enslave us into a cloned nation of mind controlled robotoids. But I will get to that later.

To jumpstart the program, they hired Edward Bernays. Bernays was the nephew of Sigmund Freud and was dubbed "the father of public relations." He wrote three books *Crystalizing Public Opinion*, *Propaganda* and *The Engineering of Consent*. Bernays believed people were so irrational and he believed so strongly in crowd psychology, that he could convince masses of people to do almost anything.

Edward Bernays was a Tavistock coach and advisor to President Woodrow Wilson. Wilson ran and won the presidency on the promise that he would keep America out of war. But with the infiltration of Bernays he persuaded Congress to declare war on Germany and started the first world war. And on December 23, 1913, while all Americans were getting ready to celebrate Christmas, Woodrow Wilson signed the Federal Reserve Act, a law that created the Federal Reserve System, the Central Banking system of the United States. This led to effectively abolishing the gold standard. It was now 1933 and Tavistock's mission was already 50% complete.

The Central bank of America was responsible for the Great Depression and the Global Financial crisis of 2007. The federal reserve violates constitutional law because their policy makers are hand-picked by people behind the federal reserve. Their meetings are secret and there is no transparency to what they are doing to the public. In 1932, an outspoken critic of the Federal Reserve, Louis T McFadden said, "We have in this country one of the most corrupt Institutions the world has ever known. I refer to the Federal Reserve Board and Bank; This evil institution has impoverished and ruined the people of the United States . . . through the corrupt practices of the money vultures who control it."

After the wars and the establishment of the central bank, America started to see moral decline through what Historians call "the new morality" or otherwise known as the birth of "liberalism". It was President Ronald Reagan that once said, "If Fascism ever come to America, it will come in the name of Liberalism." In the twenties, known as the decade of decadence, we saw the emergence of the "flapper". Women were now cursing, smoking, drinking, wearing revealing clothing and the term "loose" entered into the zeitgeist. This was a cause and effect directly from advertising and music which was pushed from Tavistock think tanks.

In the 1930's homosexuality and lesbianism became rampant, not out of any inner or latent desires but as a means to "shock" the old establishment during the great depression. During the depression, the nation was numb. GK Chesterton, a writer and philosopher said, "the moral, spiritual, racial, economic, cultural bankruptcy we are in today is not some social phenomenon but rather the outcome of a carefully planned Tavistock program."

The birth of MIT, the national institute of mental health, Stanford research center and Wharton school of economics were founded by Dr Kurt Lewin, John Rawlings Reese and Margaret Meade, arguably the best Tavistock social engineers of all time. Believe it or not, through the minds of these leaders came the brainwashing and propaganda for WW2, Vietnam, Korean war, the two gulf wars and every war that followed after.

Maurice Strong, a Canadian oil and businessman, was the president of Canada's power corporation, pushing the climate change agenda in the 1960's. What you may not know is that Maurice was also a big power player in Tavistock's social engineering machine, and he held the "conference of 1980." He gathered occult think tankers, social engineers, cybernetic experts and futurologists to discuss what "THEY" wanted to see happen in the 1980s.

Here is the list for the Tavistock conference of 1980:

- Women entering the corporate world
- Racially mixed breeding
- The rise of Oprah Winfrey to normalize mixed marriage
- Youth rebellion
- Lesbian moms
- The emergence of the fake "Green" movement
- Stressing the importance of "Meditation" and "Kabala" to confuse Christians
- The infiltration of hip-hop with gangster rap

- The new age movement

What do you think America? Were they successful in the 1980s? Amazing isn't it? Do you think it's a coincidence we started calling America the "Homeland" after 9/11? And Showtime popularized the show "Homeland"? Did you know the word "homeland" comes straight out of the Communist Manifesto?

These social scientist wizards understand you better than you understand yourself. They can profile any audience to accept lies and they know you won't even question it. Unless of course you have broken your programming. When we think of the word "intelligence" we usually think Mossad, CIA, MI6, but never do we think "Tavistock". Did you know that the majority of CIA and MI6 operatives get their training at Tavistock? Here is a list of what they learn: metaphysics, mind control, behavior modification strategy, ESP, hypnotism, esoteric knowledge, Satanism and Manichean theology, which is, understanding the duality of good and evil.

According to Dr. Coleman, the best kept secret and research that came out of Tavistock is the "Three System Response". The three-system response is how the population reacts to stress resulting from a contrived situation. "Contrived situation" is a crisis management exercises for world leaders. An example of a contrived situation was the attack on Pearl Harbor in December of 1941.

During a crisis, the first response is
1. "Superficiality" which is the condition that manifests when a group reacts to a threat by adopting shallow advertising and slogans, which they attempt to pass off as ideals. Because the cause of the crisis is not identified, it leaves the population confused and this phase can last as long as the controller wants it to.
2. The second phase is called "Fragmentation" in which panic strikes and social cohesion falls apart. This results in society to break up into small groups, all forming different attitudes and beliefs due to media manipulation. No one is on the same page, no one is getting the truth and people become divided, fragmented from each other.

This causes civil unrest, protests and verbal fights. All caused by humans failing to identify the cause of the crisis.
3. The third phase is called the "Fantasy trip". This is what Tavistock calls dissociation. In this last phase of the psychological operation, people have been so traumatized from the false flag event they block it out, lose interest and all hope in humanity. This dissociation causes people to allow their liberties to get taken away which ushers in communist legislation without a fight.

Julius Caesar once said, "Divide and conquer". The powers that be have been using contrived situations and false flag events to shock and traumatize the world since the beginning of time. The JFK assassination, Waco, OJ Simpson car chase, Columbine, 9/11, Sandy Hook, Orlando shooting, Las Vegas shooting…And don't even get me started on crisis actors. You can research that one.

Do you think all of these shootings at schools, post offices, churches, concerts and shopping malls were just coincidence? According to Dr. Coleman they were carried out by mind-controlled subjects who were carefully profiled, sought after and put on dangerous, mood altering drugs like Ritalin and controlled by DARPA computer programmers.

Remember the national story about Molly Tibbets, the jogger who disappeared for a month and was found dead in a cornfield from Iowa? At first her alleged killer said he "heard voices in his head", and the media had a hay day with him saying that. Now you cannot find that anywhere on the internet. Did you know Mollie Tibbets dad was an architect for the Clinton Foundation? He actually designed the orphanages in Haiti. Also, just do a quick internet search of "killers who hear voices" and it is astonishing. I also recommend the book "programmed to kill" by David McGowan.

When I think about what has happened to women in America it is easy to see how it has been done in hindsight. From the flappers to pornography, we can see that Tavistock is really good at what they do. Remember 50 shades of grey? This was another mind control experiment that you could do in your own bedroom. The pain and fear that comes with sadomasochistic sex causes the brain to shunt blood flow away from its executive decision-making areas (frontal cortex), which results in an altered state of consciousness in both the giver and the receiver. Like doing cocaine. Do you ever wonder why certain books or movies get propped up? This always raises a red flag for me.

Herbert Hoover was the 31st president of the United States. He was a republican and was reluctant to become involved with the Federal Reserve. He believed in strengthening American business and believed that individual reliance on banks would weaken the economy. There is speculation from Coleman that his reluctance caused the Stock Market crash of 1929, which led America into the great depression, as a punishment to him and the American people.

Tavistock engineered the Cuban Missile crisis as an attempt to sell the FEMA program to JFK. It was another rejection by Kennedy, and he died that same year. Tavistock immediately signed a contract with NASA to ramp up public opinion on "space." Ronald Reagan was another president who was reluctant to fall in line and there was an assassination attempt on him. During Reagan's presidency the Committee had a secret meeting to make sure after this presidency, they remained in control with their candidates of choice.

George Herbert Walker bush was the next in line. He was former director of the CIA and the Vice President to Reagan. He was a member of Skull and Bones at Yale and was married to Barbara Bush, who keeps fetuses in jars in her home and who is allegedly Aelister Crowley's daughter by a striking resemblance. Bush gave the famous New World Order speech following the Gulf war of 91. Next, we had Rhodes scholar Bill Clinton, then George W Bush and then Obama. With these presidents came more social engineering, false flags and corruption at the highest levels.

John Coleman once said, "We have been brainwashed into believing that Communism is the greatest danger we Americans are facing. This is simply not so. The greatest danger arises from the mass of traitors in our midst. Our Constitution warns us to be watchful of the enemy within our gates. These enemies are the servants of the Committee of 300 who occupy high positions within our governmental structure. The UNITED STATES is where we MUST begin our fight to turn back the tide threatening to engulf us, and where we must meet, and defeat these internal conspirators."

Trump has been the most difficult for Tavistock. He was discussed in a couple of Tavistock journals written by James Mackay, the director for Tavistock coaching. In 2016, He expressed concern that based on Trump's personality, he would be very difficult to "coach" and in 2018, he discussed how Trump is like a "trickster." Is this a confession that Trump hasn't fallen in line but has been steps ahead of the committee?

Another modern goal of the committee of 300 is the emergence of the "technotronic era". In the book "Between two ages" by Brzezinski he says, "The technotronic era involves the gradual appearance of a more controlled society. Such a society would be dominated by an elite, unrestrained by traditional values. Soon it will be possible to assert almost continuous surveillance over every citizen and maintain up-to-date complete files containing even the most personal information about the citizen. These files will be subject to instantaneous retrieval by the authorities." That's creepy.

And who is his daughter, Mika Brzezinski, the talk show host on Morning Joe, with Joe Scarborough. This is the guy Trump accused of murdering one of his staffers. The book by Brzezinski also discussed future human cloning and "robotoids", people who acted like people and who seemed to be people, but who were not. I just want to point out that everyone thinks Elon Musk is cool but he's also pushing for normalization of the Neuralink brain chip and in my opinion, this is not something we should be excited about.

The Beatles might be one of the biggest psychological operations ever played on the world. The Beatles were part of the counter-culture, pushing rock music and LSD in the 1960's. The baby boomers fell in love with them along with the Rolling Stones, Bob Dylan and other folk artists of the time. What people may not know is there was a man by the name of Theodore Adorno who allegedly wrote all of the Beatles songs. Theodore was born in 1903 and died in 1969, right before the Beatles broke up in 1970. According to the Brazilian president, Jair Bolsonaro, he claimed that the Beatles were a terrible band that could hardly play their instruments.

He claimed they were semi-illiterate when it came to music. When the Beatles catalog was put up for sale and purchased by Michael Jackson, there was much ado about why Paul McCartney was not able to own them himself. This is because Paul did not own the rights to the music that he, himself did not write. Theodor Adorno's estate owned the songs. It was the estate of Adorno that sold the catalog to Michael Jackson.

John Lennon knew about the corruption and was completely aware of what was going on. He knew what he was a part of and started voicing his opinion about it. He called the men who controlled the world "psychopaths" and in return was called a "loose cannon". During a Playboy interview, Lennon discussed the unforeseen liberal impact LSD was having on human civilization and that the powers that be were up to massive social manipulation schemes. We all know the fate of Lennon didn't last long when he was gunned down in front of his apartment by a Manchurian candidate, Mark David Chapman, ordered by George H.W. Bush. It has been written that the CIA forced the Yoko Ono to keep gravitating Lennon towards the "social fringe" and she was a programmed multiple herself.

Today, people are still distracted with what the elite call the "Bread and circuses" of baseball, football, endless Hollywood and social security. Nothing has changed. The program is so good, if you were to try and explain this to someone, they would think you are crazy. That is how good the programming is. Because after all, if you don't program your mind, someone will program it for you. And it makes me remember the Tavistock whistleblower, Arthur Cherep-Spiridovich, the man who took his own life at the age of 59. Or did he? Did he know too much? In 2021, looking back it seems to me that he knew a lot.

Tavistock Institute is unique because it has the independence of being entirely self-financing, with no subsidies from the government or other sources; the action research orientation places it between, but not in, the worlds of academia and consultancy; and its range of disciplines include anthropology, economics, organizational behavior, political science, psychoanalysis, psychology and sociology.

The ideology of American foundations was created by the Tavistock

Institute of Human Relations in London. In 1921, the Duke of Bedford, Marquess of Tavistock, the 11th Duke, gave a building to the Institute to study the effect of shellshock on British soldiers who survived World War I. Its purpose was to establish the "breaking point" of men under stress, under the direction of the British Army Bureau of Psychological Warfare, commanded by Sir John Rawlings-Reese.

When American Evangelist E. Grandison Finney became a minister, he realized he needed to create a disturbing sermon through fear, shock and emotion to heighten suggestibility in his people. Finney began to deliver sermons loudly, filled with emotion and this was the birth of Evangelism. It also became known as the "Boston Movement", exemplified in hysterical rants which made it very clear these men were more interested in making a dollar than actually helping anyone. Finney's techniques inspired the creation of the Children of God church in the 1960's.

The **Children of God** cult promoted pedophilia and mind control. The Children of God cult was protected by Chilean dictator Pinochet at the time. River and Joaquin Phoenix were members of this cult as children. River revealed as a child that he was forced to have sex with adults when he was just four years old. Rose McGowan and Julian Assange were also victims of this cult as children.

Another cult group called **The Family** (in Australia) was created by Anne Hamilton-Byrne. Anne claimed to be the reincarnation of Jesus Christ living under a master who came to Earth. The children who were under her supervision were frequently dosed with psychiatric drugs and isolated from each other. This technique is reminiscent of MK ULTRA, PROJECT MONARCH and other CIA controlled illegal experiments. Interestingly enough, Julian Assange was a member when he was a child.

Psychologist, Sigmond Freud, settled in Maresfield Gardens when he moved to England. He was given a mansion by Princess Bonaparte. Tavistock's pioneer work in behavioral science along Freudian lines of "controlling" humans established it as the world center of foundation ideology. Tavistock's network is now extended through Stanford Research Institute, MIT, Hudson Institute, Center of Strategic and International Studies, Esalen and the Heritage Foundation. The Center of Strategic and

International Studies at Georgetown is where members of the state department, US Air Force, Rand and Mitre corporation personnel are required to undergo indoctrination under the Tavistock institute.

Two other secret groups the American Ditchley Foundation and Mont Pelerin Society are conduits for instructions to the Tavistock network.

Statue of Sigmund Freud at Tavistock Institute of mind control

The Tavistock Institute developed the mass brain-washing techniques which were first used on American prisoners of war in Korea. These brain-washing techniques have been widely used on the public in efforts to modify individual behavior through topical psychology. Kurt Lewin, a German, became director of Tavistock in 1932. He came to the U.S. in 1933 as a "refugee", the first of many infiltrators, and set up the Harvard Psychology Clinic, which originated the propaganda campaign to turn the American public against Germany and involve us in World War II.

In 1938, Roosevelt executed a secret agreement with Churchill which in effect ceded U.S. sovereignty to England, because it agreed to let Special Operations Executive control U.S. policies.
To implement this agreement, Roosevelt sent General Donovan to London for indoctrination before setting up the Office of Strategic Services (OSS and now the CIA) under the aegis of SOE-SIS. The entire OSS program, as well as the CIA has always worked on guidelines set up by the Tavistock Institute.

Tavistock Institute originated the mass civilian bombing raids carried out by Roosevelt and Churchill purely as a clinical experiment in mass terror, keeping records of the results as they watched the "guinea pigs" react under "controlled laboratory conditions". All Tavistock and American foundation techniques have a single goal---to break down the psychological strength of the individual and force them to surrender to the New World Order.

The methods of Freudian psychotherapy induce permanent mental illness in those who undergo this treatment by destabilizing their character. The victim is then advised to "establish new rituals of personal interaction", that is, to indulge in brief sexual encounters which actually set the participants adrift with no stable personal relationships in their lives, destroying their ability to establish or maintain a family. Another prominent Tavistock operation is the Wharton School of Finance at the University of Pennsylvania. They are also connected with NASA.

The infamous MK Ultra program involved dosing unsuspecting citizens with LSD and their adverse reactions were studied as if they were "guinea pigs". These experiments resulted in mental illness and death. All of this information came out, trials were had but there was no justice to what had been done. Sandoz AG, a Swiss drug company, developed LSD and this company was owned by S.G. Warburg. Roosevelt's advisor, James Paul Warburg, was the son of Paul Warburg who wrote the Federal Reserve Act and helped set up Tavistock. See how this all connects?

Another key component to Tavistock is the Ditchley Foundation, founded in 1957. The American branch of Ditchley is run by the Rockefellers and the Council on Foreign Relations. They are dubbed "through the looking glass", interesting nickname I would say. Tavistock was created and operated solely for the purpose to bring in a new world order over the American people. The Rockefeller Foundation also has its tentacles in controlling world agriculture. They control programs throughout Mexico and Latin America. The independent farmer is a threat to the New World Order.

There are many Tavistock institutions in the United States. Some of them are Flow laboratories, Merle Thomas Corporation, Walden Research,

Planning Research Corporation, Brookings Institute, Hudson Institute, National Training Laboratories, University of Pennsylvania (Wharton School of Finance), Institute for Social Research and Institute for the Future.

Stanford Research Institute was founded in 1946 with a goal to research mind control and science. They were behind the "Aquarius" conspiracies starting in the 1960's and many powerful corporations sought out their services. Some of them were Bank of America, Wells Fargo, Hewlett Packard and the TRW Company. Other companies that are connected to Stanford are MIT, Harvard, UCLA, Rand Corporation, U.S. Army and the Office of Naval Intelligence.

The **Institute for Policy Studies** (IPS) has been responsible for shaping United States policies (domestic and foreign) and was founded by James Warburg and the Rothschild family. They are all about the "new left" movements we see so dominantly on the world stage. It has been written they were the true force behind the Black Panthers and powerful lobbyists.

Massachusetts Institute of Technology (MIT) is a massive institution but rarely recognized as being under the Tavistock umbrella. MIT and other groups (which I will name shortly) are responsible for funding Uniform Law Foundation whose main function is to ensure that Uniform Commercial Code (UCC) remains the true process for how businesses operate in the United States. The UCC falls under maritime law and the Holy See of the Vatican. See how this all connects? Some of these groups that oversee this are Systems Dynamic, NASA, U.S. Army, U.S. Department of State, U.S. Navy, U.S. Treasury and Volkswagen, to name a few.

The **Rand Corporation** is a non-profit think tank created in 1948 by Douglas Aircraft company to analyze the United States Armed Forces. It is one of the closest allies to Tavistock. Some of Rand's clients have included AT&T, Chase Bank, International Business Machines (IBM), National Science Foundation, TRW, United States Air Force, United States Department of Energy, United States Department of Health to name a few. Brainwashing, indoctrination and mind control are the soul reasons the Rand Corporation exists.

WORLD ECONOMIC FORUM

"You will own nothing and be happy." – Klaus Schwab, 2020

In the 1940s, B.F. Skinner, a behavioral psychologist claimed that children could be conditioned and trained rather than "educated", like animals. in the traditional sense. His ideas were considered extremely radical, at least back then.

Using simple rewards and punishments to encourage and discourage behaviors, Skinner experimented with animals inside a Skinner Boxes. A Skinner Box had levers and bars and each time the animal would press the right lever or bar the animal would receive food or drink. If the animal did not do what Skinner did, the animal would be punished through electric shock. It was basically a form of MK ULTRA for animals.

After enough of the conditioning with "programmed instruction" through "teaching machines," the animal learned to do exactly what the scientist wanted. The goal had been achieved: It was possible to scientifically modify behavior of an animal through a process called "Operant Conditioning." Conditioning. This is what the Mayor of Chicago, Lori Lightfoot always says. Conditioning. Eventually, BF Skinner could predict behavior, too.

Skinner theorized that, like animals, children could also be conditioned because he started to view humans as nothing but biological stimulus-response machines. And his next frontier was to find out whether children's attitudes, values and beliefs could be manipulated too. Now, today, the same methods are used, but instead of a Skinner box, today's methods include computers, algorithms and AI. Computers and AI offer fun sounds and images, while social media for kids and adults offer the dose of dopamine each time, they get a like or comment on their photograph.

And now we have the looming Great Reset which is basically funded by the United Nations, World Economic Forum and the International Monetary

Fund or what I call the Black Nobility, to essentially institute global feudalism. A one world government. The New World Order. The Leader of this movement or the Black Nobility's puppet is Klaus Schwab.

Klaus Schwab said back in June of 2020 that all aspects of our social and economic life must be revamped and the growing alliance with companies like Microsoft, Zoom and Google are being relied on more than ever before. Said more simply, in the brave new COVID19 virus world of "education," teachers will no longer be teachers—glorified babysitters, perhaps, but not educators in the traditional sense. Computers and algorithms will become the true teachers. E-learning will be the new norm.

My background is eLearning. I used to create eLearning for corporations years ago before I quit forever. Now, eLearning was meant to be for adults only. It's something you do alone and online. It was for adults who worked and didn't have much time or money to go to school. Then it was implemented in companies for training purposes like sexual harassment and things like that. It was never supposed to be intended for children. And now I feel like this was all part of the great reset plan.

Klaus Schwab described all of us as being in "confinement" that's the word he uses to describe our lockdown. And the powers that be are taking advantage of us being home right now because they know we are becoming more dependent on the internet for literally everything this year. Klaus Schwab was talking about smart toilets, ok, saying he wants them rolled out to track our health data and perform health analysis.

And what gets creepier is that he talks about the "Fourth Industrial Revolution," which will lead to "a fusion of our physical, digital and biological identity." And now this rapid spread of Orwellian technology is conditioning us all into potential transhuman robots. We know companies have already gobbled up plenty of data, just think what they are doing now with children and their iPads and smart tech. And they want this AI to act as a teacher. And I think the main question we all should be asking is, who is programming this Artificial Intelligence? Is the AI being programmed by a God-fearing liberty minded American Patriot or a complete psychopath? I would put my money on the psychopath.

There has been a reemergence of these dancing nurses and doctors I mean what is going on. What is wrong with these people? Who in their right mind agrees to participate in such a low-level shenanigans? And some people are saying that maybe the nurses are dancing to expose the hoax, to discredit the mainstream narrative. And that could very well be true, but why not just hold a press conference? Why the obnoxious dancing. It is just insanity to me.

The World Economic Forum is based in Switzerland and is an International Non-Governmental Organization (NGO) and was founded on January 24th, 1971 by Klaus Schwab. The group meets annually in Davos, Switzerland to discuss business, politics, academics and how to shape global, regional and industry agendas. To get a badge for entry requires a membership to the World Economic Forum, which costs somewhere between $60,000 and $600,000, plus an additional fee of more than $27,000 per person to get into the conference itself. There are 3,000 people who are invited each year but only 2/3 show up to attend the full conference.

According to Elmira Bayrasli, "Davos is a family reunion for the people who broke the modern world." Wow. What an interesting quote. According to Craig Murray and ex-British ambassador turned human rights activist says, Davos serves as nothing but an annual reminder of how very poorly 'God' aims avalanches." Christine Lagarde from the International Monetary Fund once said, "rising economic inequality is not a recipe for stability and sustainability."

Jonathan Cook, journalist, wrote, "their long experiment in liberalism has finally run its course. Liberalism has patently failed and failed catastrophically. These intellects are standing, like the rest of us, on a precipice from which we are about to jump or topple." Liberalism is being rejected in many forms but when does the house of cards fall?

Liberalism is a deeply flawed ideology and to some a religion. It is idolatry of a hellish value system set out to destroy the world. If you look into the current trends and agendas on the world stage you will find yourself staring back at the United Nation's Agenda 2030, The Paris Climate Agreement, the Fourth Industrial Revolution and the Bank for

International Settlement of 2025. These agendas give you a glimpse into the mind of the elites and how they want to turn our lives inside out over the course of the next decade. Will we let them?

COVID19 has dominated the news and our lives since March of 2020. COVID19 is the trojan horse to show humans what life will be like after the virus is "over". After the Communists locked us down in March of 2020, details of the Great Reset started to pour out. Three months prior to the COVID19 scamdemic, "Event 201" was held in New York which was a simulated outlook of a virus that spread from Brazil. The event concluded that the pandemic would continue until 80-90% of the population is exposed or there is a vaccine. Not only did this event explain that a massive amount of the human population will die but we will see catastrophic social and economic changes following the pandemic.

Event 201 was held by the World Economic Forum, the Bill and Melinda Gates Foundation and the Johns Hopkins Center. John Hopkins established a Coronavirus Resource Center which was the 'go to' source for global infections. Bill Gates, eugenicist, has been talking about depopulating the planet via Ted Talks since 2010 and has been a driving force in the vaccine world for decades.

The World Economic Forum has six partners, and they are Johnson & Johnson, NBC, Edelman Communications, Marriott International, Henry Schein and Bill and Melinda Gates Foundation. These partnerships were formed to ensure the group's agendas were put into place and executed. It is important to mention some of the members of the Board of Trustees Fabiola Gianotta (director of CERN), Queen Rania of Jordan, Al Gore, Jack Ma, Mark Schneider (CEO of Nestle), Christine Lagarde, Lawrence Fink (CEO of BlackRock and Trilateral Commission) and other influential people from France, Japan, China, United States, India and Singapore to name a few.

The World Economic Forum is always looking for new members by joining the New Champions Community. A 12-month membership is $24,000 and some of the co-curators are Yale University, Oxford University (home of the Rhodes scholarship), MIT, Harvard, Imperial

College of London, and the Council on Foreign Relations. MIT published an article back in March 2019 that was titled "We're not going back to normal" and proclaimed that social distancing is here to stay. The World Economic Forum has what they call 'Content Partners' who analyze over 1,000 articles a day from think tanks and research institutes. Some of these partners include Brookings Institute, Council on Foreign Relations, Rand Corporation, Cambridge University, Harvard University and the Royal Institute of Royal Affairs.

The World Economic Forum has a group of Young Global Leaders which consists of 800 people chosen by the organizers to represent the organization. After five years they are considered alumni. Guess who are the World Economic Forum's "Young Global Leaders" of 2020? Alicia Garza, founder of Black Lives Matter. And Jesús Cepeda, CEO of One Smart City, pushing Agenda 2030 and bringing artificial intelligence to cities. Shocker. Other notable members of the World Economic Forum's "Young Leaders" are Gavin Newsom, Sergei Brin, Zuckerberg, Larry Page, Jack Ma, Ashton Kutcher, Leo DiCaprio, Charlize Theron, Priyanka Chopra, Gavin Newsom, Eric Schmidt, etc.

The World Economic Forum has hosted the following platforms:

- COVID19 Action Platform
- Shaping the Future of Technology Governance: Blockchain and Distributed Ledger Technologies
- Shaping the Future of the New Economy and Society
- Shaping the Future of Consumption
- Shaping the Future of Digital Economy and New Value Creation
- Shaping the Future of Financial and Monetary Systems
- Shaping the Future of Technology Governance: Artificial Intelligence and Machine Learning
- Shaping the Future of Trade and Global Economic Interdependence
- Shaping the Future of Cities, Infrastructure and Urban Services
- Shaping the Future of Energy and Materials

- Shaping the Future of Media, Entertainment and Culture

When you google Klaus Schwab books, you get seven, dating back to 2002. He has written about reshaping Asia, the fourth industrial revolution and the great reset. And by now you have probably seen his creepy videos discussing food shortages, lockdowns, and amenities granted for those who have received the COVID19 vaccine. Klaus Schwab is one of the puppets for the Black Nobility. He wrote the Davos Manifesto of 2020 and it is online for anyone to read but it basically states that there is a conflict over the future of capitalism and the future of technology. And this all ties into Social media companies, censorship, 5G and artificial intelligence (agendas of the Trilateral Commission). By now you can connect all the dots and see that none of this is coincidence.

To add some historical context to the World Economic Forum, it was originally founded at the European Management Forum. You could say this group was created as an extension of the Trilateral Commission to widen its reach in economic and social issues worldwide. The World Economic Forum describes themselves as being a 'catalyst for global initiatives' aka the Great Reset/Fourth Industrial Revolution.

The World Economic Forum is all about the technological revolution, science advancement and climate change/sustainable development. They have said, "over the next decade, we will witness changes tearing through the global economy with an unprecedented speed, scale and force." They are committed nurturing their agenda until it goes through. In the World Economic Forum's own words, "success is measured not only in terms of immediate results - we understand that real progress takes time and sustained commitment."

PHI BETA KAPPA

"We know what we are but know not what we may be."

Phi Beta Kappa was the first fraternity in the United States and was established by the Jesuits at the college of William and Mary. Its purpose was to include honorary members who would go on to be involved in government and to "shape" the country. In the 1960's, Vanderbilt professor Donald Davidson claimed that Phi Beta Kappa was a Marxist fraternity and heavily influenced by communist ideals.

Six out of the nine Supreme Court Justices that sit on the Supreme Court are Phi Beta Kappa. Is it a coincidence that some of the worst presidents (arguably) were Phi Beta Kappa? Some of them include George H.W. Bush, Bill Clinton, Woodrow Wilson (who sold the United States out to the Rothschild banking dynasty), Jimmy Carter, and Franklin Pierce (who set the stage for the civil war).

Other members include Chuck Schumer, Adam Schiff, Tim Kaine, Richard Blumenthal, Nelson Rockefeller, Henry Kissinger, Clive Davis, Gloria Steinem, Kris Kristofferson (monarch handler), Lynn Cheney, Barack Obama Sr., Francis Ford Coppola, Michio Kaku, Jeb Bush, George Stephanopoulos, Jeff Bezos, Fred Rogers, Kellyanne Conway, Pete Buttigieg, Ben Shapiro, Eliot Spitzer, Dinesh D'Souza, Heidi Cruz, Barbara Bush, John Rockefeller, Ashley Judd, Peyton Manning, Rivers Cuomo, Condoleezza Rice, Amanpour and James Holmes (the 2012 Aurora, Colorado shooter).

James Holmes has been dubbed an American mass murderer, but I call him a Manchurian candidate. Holmes was raised in California, ran cross country and tried to commit suicide at age 11. According to Holmes, he was tormented by what he called "nail ghosts" who would hammer on the walls at night. He also claimed he would see shadows and light flickers in the corner of his eyes. His psychiatrist once said he was "obsessed with killing for over a decade." Holmes went to college at the University of

California, Riverside in 2010 where he received a Bachelor of Science degree in neuroscience with top honors. He was a member of **Phi Beta Kappa**.

His father, Robert Holmes, was a Stanford scientist with a Master's in biostatistics. Robert Holmes patented a predictive model system that is used to detect telecommunications fraud. It is clear to see that Holmes is a victim of MKULTRA or some other brainwashing project. Holmes was charged with 24 counts of murder in the first degree and 140 counts of attempted murder. He is facing 12 life sentences in prison without possibility of parole.

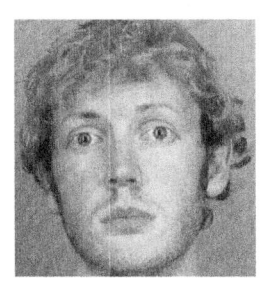

James Holmes

The Supreme Court of the United States is the highest court in the federal judiciary system, but it is the Society of Jesus, the Jesuits who are in control of them. Members of the Supreme Court hold secret ranks within the Jesuit system. Some are connected to Black Nobility some are members of the Council on Foreign Relations and others are part of military orders that gives complete allegiance to the pope. The Jesuits control the world's finance, the press, entertainment, intelligence agencies and governments of the world.

Here is a rundown of who sits on the Supreme Court of the United States.

Stephen Breyer – Liberal Jew – Appointed by Bill Clinton – Stanford – **Phi Beta Kappa** – Magdalen College (House of Orange) – Married Joanna Freda Hare (Black Nobility) – Served as the fact checker for the Warren Commission – Member of the Council on Foreign Relations

Clarence Thomas – Conservative – Appointed by George H.W. Bush – College of the Holy Cross (Jesuit) – Alpha Sigma Nu – Skeleton Key Society – Involved in the Anita Hill scandal (Humiliation ritual)

John G. Roberts – Conservative - Appointed by George W. Bush – Catholic – Harvard – Served in the justice department during Reagan admin – **Phi Beta Kappa** – obsessed with "Marxism & Bolshevism" – Professor at Jesuit Georgetown University – Name was on Jeffrey Epstein flight log

Amy Coney Barrett – Conservative - Appointed by Donald Trump - Catholic – Notre Dame/Rhodes – **Phi Beta Kappa** – Rutgers - her father, Michael Coney, was a career lawyer for Rothschild Shell Oil Company

Samuel Alito – Conservative - Appointed by George W. Bush - **Phi Beta Kappa** – Princeton/Yale – Assistant Attorney General in justice department under Edwin Meese

Neil Gorsuch – Conservative - Appointed by Trump – Georgetown Jesuit Prep School – **Phi Beta Kappa** – Colombia/Harvard – Classmate of Barack Obama at Harvard – Oxford (Married a Brit)

Sonia Sotomayor – Ultraliberal – Appointed by Barack Obama – Catholic – Princeton/Yale – **Phi Beta Kappa** – Worked under Mario Cuomo and Ed Koch

Elena Kagan – Liberal - Appointed by Barack Obama – Princeton/Oxford/Harvard – Thesis was about her strong interest in "Socialism" – Met Barack Obama at the University of Chicago Law – Served as the Dean at Harvard

Brett Kavanaugh – Conservative - Appointed by Trump - Georgetown Jesuit Prep School – Yale – Delta Kappa Epsilon – Legal Team of George W Bush – Christine Blasey Ford (humiliation ritual) Married George W. Bush's personal secretary

Now that I have broken down the power structure of the world stage, it is easy to see how all of the wars, epidemics and false flags have managed to happen almost seamlessly to no avail, throughout history. It is a rude awakening when you wake up and realize that almost everything you know is a lie. It is a rude awakening to realize that everything you have been taught about history has been hidden.

It is a harsh one to swallow but once you are awake to the madness you can break free. Once the veil is lifted you no longer have to live with limits. Stop living outside your means. Don't keep up with the Jones'. Get out of debt. Stop being their slave. Be authentic. Stop caring what others think about you. Release yourself from the mental and financial chains of this 3D matrix world. Learn to be truly happy and find peace within yourself.

There are powerful men and women who are working to change society as they see fit. They are pushing agendas and technology using mind control to modify our behavior. They want to keep us distracted, break up our families and keep us dumbed down so they can implement these plans worldwide. We can resist. The key is knowledge. The key is knowing the plan and knowing the players. We can fight this and the more people that wake up the better.

Hope is not lost. This world needs prayer now more than ever. Stay positive, keep red and black pilling your friends and family and stay vigilant. I will leave you with that to do your own critical thinking. Until then, stay safe out there and don't stop questioning the world around you.

Printed in Great Britain
by Amazon